Minting

A New Selection of Ted Walker's Poetry

Edited by Diana Barsham and Ross Hair

University of Chichester

First published 2010-08-20
by University of Chichester
http://www.chiuni.ac.uk

Printed in Great Britain by
MWL Print Group, Pontypool, South Wales

The action is one of the most beautiful movements in sport. Performing it perfectly is deeply satisfying. All the muscles from the toes to fingertips have to be precisely co-ordinated. The small throwing circle imposes a stringent discipline. From stillness, within a bare second, the thrower uncoils to attain maximum acceleration. Strength and speed – controlled – engender grace. ... I trained in a kind of tranced obsession, loving the parabola of flight which resulted if – perhaps once in every five attempts – I got everything right. The discus, metal rim glinting, rode the air its few marvelous instants, spinning upon itself but not wobbling, catching the sun.

The High Path, *Ted Walker*

'My birthday morning mints a sun'

Birthday Song

Minting the Sun

Contents

Introduction

"Tendrils of Flame": The Poetry of Ted Walker

Compared to many other poets, Ted Walker's poetry career started relatively late. He had already turned thirty and was Head of Modern Languages at Bognor Grammar School when his first major book, *Fox on a Barn Door*, was published by Jonathan Cape in 1965. For a debut collection, however, the book met with considerable praise. The noted British poet Ian Hamilton called Walker "the real thing" in *The Spectator* and P. N. Furbank, writing in *The Listener*, praised Walker as "a brilliant performer" possessing "a most seductive Tennysonian delicacy."[i] A. Alvarez, in an enthusiastic review in *The Observer*, praised *Fox on a Barn Door* as "a collection of considerable achievement and even greater promise."[ii] Indeed, Alvarez was true to his word about Walker's "great promise" and, one year later, included him in his anthology *The New Poetry* which profiled Walker alongside more established names, including Sylvia Plath, Philip Larkin, and Thom Gunn. Walker also received positive reviews on the other side of the Atlantic, no doubt, partly due to his poems being regularly featured in *The New Yorker*. M. L. Rosenthal, for example, in *The New York Times Book Review,* wrote approvingly of Walker's achievements believing that "Seldom has a young poet's first volume crackled with such acute perceptions."[iii]

For a first collection a poet could not ask for more a positive reception. However, what is even more remarkable is that, by his own admission, Walker was largely self-taught, apprenticing himself to a small number of poets. In one of the few critical essays on Walker, published in the prestigious literary periodical *The Southern Review*, John Press writes that, "Walker insists that his knowledge of English poetry at the outset of his career as a poet was small. The major formative influence was Ted Hughes, and Walker owed a great deal also to Robert Frost." Press adds that Walker's "great love is John Clare" and "among contemporaries, he finds most sustenance in Philip Larkin, Robert Lowell, and Leslie Norris."[iv] These influences are valuable for beginning to understand and assess Walker's poetry in more detail and give a sense of where Walker falls within the scope of post-war British poetry, as well as indicating some of his poetry's principle thematic concerns and formal techniques.

First and foremost, Walker is a local poet who takes significant place in a rich tradition of Sussex poetry.[v] The Welsh poet, Leslie Norris, who lived in nearby Aldingbourne and was headmaster of Westergate School—and, later, a lecturer at the Bognor Regis College of Education (now part of the University of Chichester)—was an important friend and influence for Walker. Andrew Young, a Scottish poet and clergyman who moved to Sussex in 1920, later becoming the Vicar of Stonegate and a Canon of Chichester Cathedral, was another. Included in the present volume is Walker's touching elegy "For Andrew Young" in which Walker warmly refers to Young as a "close, / Remote, loved, unknowable companion." The rural Sussex environs became a prominent theme in both these older poets' work, Norris and Young, and encouraged the regional bent of Walker's own writing. This is particularly evident in the poem, "For John Charles Walker, Killed on Shoreham Beach," from *The Night Bathers* which alludes to a number of local features of the Sussex port town of Shoreham-by-Sea, including the Marlipins pub (which can still be found in the town) and the Adur, the Sussex river that reaches the English Channel at Shoreham. Overlooking the English Channel, Shoreham-by-Sea was also a place of strategic importance in World War Two. Thus, in the advent of enemy invasion, landmines were laid on the beach as a defensive measure. It was a landmine that killed the poem's subject, John Charles Walker, Walker's paternal uncle, as he "strolled to pinch firewood / From the one innocent house that still stood / On Shoreham beach."[vi] Evidently, this coastal "booby-trap" made a considerable impression on the young Walker, as it also informs his earlier poem "Breakwaters," from *Fox on A Barn Door*. In his interview with Clive Wilmer, Walker explains that he "wasn't allowed to play on [the beach] because it was war time and the beach was a minefield":

> And on stormy days we'd often hear the mines exploding. So when I finally walked on that beach at the age of 11, the sound of the sea smashing against the breakwaters was linked with the sound of those explosions and the whole scene seemed terribly important to me. So when twenty years later I came to write a poem called 'Breakwaters,' I was really writing about that early experience.[vii]

In addition to cultural and historical landmarks, Walker's regional scope also encompasses the flora, fauna, and topography of his Sussex environs. As well as Young and Andrews, it is also possible to see Walker following in the tradition of his "great love," the Romantic poet John Clare. However, Ian Hamilton believes that Walker's "regional self-consciousness" has "taken a lead" from Ted Hughes's "preoccupation with vanishing or threatened forms of English life."[viii] Indeed, as the "other" Ted, Hughes has cast a considerable shadow over Walker's work. Reviews of *Fox on a Barn Door*, in particular, proliferate with comparisons to Hughes, although his influence extends well beyond Walker's debut collection. Rosenthal, for example, writes:

> The influence of Ted Hughes, England's most powerful poet to emerge since World War II, on Ted Walker seems obvious. The very title of his first book, "Fox on a Barn Door," is reminiscent of Hughes, and so are his subjects in poems like "Porpoises," "The Skate Fishers" and "Carp." Though gentler than Hughes, and closer sometimes to sentimentality, Walker has a similar muscular precision of phrasing and movement, and his poems can recall the rank menagerie, reeking of blood, of Hughes's imagination.[ix]

Rosenthal's comparison is a perceptive one, particularly with regard to Walker's "muscular precision of phrasing and movement." Walker demonstrates an innovative use of strong stresses and alliteration very much reminiscent of Hughes's earlier work such as *The Hawk in the Rain*. And, like Hughes, Walker often invokes the accentual and alliterative force of Anglo-Saxon verse—*Beowulf*, for example, or "The Sea Fairer"—and Gerard Manley Hopkins's sprung rhythms and consonantal internal rhymes. Take, for example, the opening stanza of "With Weasel" from *The Solitaries*:

> Crevice of a soft-rot wall,
> the rib-cage of a carcase,
> stump crumble, a kingfisher's hole –
> anywhere housing foulness
> suits. Once from a hulk of pike[x]

There is also, perhaps, an echo here of the "unabashed *bravura* of alliteration, and the elaborately cunning metre" that characterises Thomas Hardy's best verse.[xi] Indeed,

Hardy is another poet whose regional sensibilities and self-taught prosodic "audacities" prefigure Walker's work.[xii] Each stanza of "With Weasel," for example, comprises five enjambed lines that conform to a strict count of seven syllables. This "syllabic verse" can at times, Martin Seymour Smith suggests in his review of *The Solitaries*, make the poems "rather gormless" and diminish the opportunity for a more spontaneous or dynamic prosody.[xiii] More often than not, however, this rudimentary syllabic count is something that Walker uses to full effect. In "Weasel" it is combined with some strong alliteration— reminiscent of Hughes—that creates an effect of compression especially apt for such a lithe and cunning subject as the weasel. Walker exploits some hard "c" sounds, evident in "*C*revice," "*c*age," "*c*arcase," "*c*rumble," "*k*ingfisher," "hul*k*" and "pi*k*e," offsetting them with some equally emphatic assonance: the "o" in "s*o*ft-r*o*t," for example, and "u" of "st*u*mp cr*u*mble" and "h*u*lk." The result of this is a tangible and palpable sensation. Reading this poem it is possible to feel the supple, ermine contours of this mammal lithely squeezing itself through the poem's solid, inflexible words. It is no mean feat that Walker so deftly creates out of them a dwelling for the creature every bit as habitable as carcass, crevice, or wall.

Frequently taking the natural world as his principle subject, it is possible to see Hughes's influence in this aspect of Walker's poetry too. However, as Rosenthal notes, Walker's poems tend to be "gentler than Hughes, and closer sometimes to sentimentality." Where Hughes's natural world is often a brute, feral, and violent one, Walker's wildness is a tamer affair. According to Peter Porter, Walker lacks the shamanic empathy that Hughes shares with his non-human subjects. "Walker is an unrepentant celebrator of the tamed South of England," Porter writes: "Apparent similarities to Ted Hughes in his early poems were misleading: Walker has no taste for shamanism."[xiv] Indeed, there is a discernible Larkinesque emphasis on seeing things as they are that curbs Walker's tendencies toward both Hughes's shamanism and the more overtly visionary Romantic epiphanies of a Wordsworth or Coleridge. Walker frequently presents a persona in his poems of the simple, ordinary, family man. The speaker in "Sunday Drive to the Beach," for example, comes across as a modest, unassuming, and unpretentious father who "shake[s] off the failed week" while his children forget him whilst, "In comic pursuit of their salt crazed dog."

Indeed, Walker's world is very much a domestic and familial one. The South Downs may very well be "numinous hills" for Walker, as he writes in *The High Path*, but the cultivated space of his own garden becomes an equally potent place for reflection and insight.[xv] This is evident in Walker's poem "Ivy," in *Burning the Ivy*, which describes the poet's attempt to manage his garden. Cutting, hacking, and burning the ivy that "swarms the ancient wall" of his garden plot, the poet finds in this tenacious plant a pertinent manifestation of the obfuscated "ravaging roots" of human memory and emotion—the "dust of dead seasons," the "tangle of years"—that, left untended, "gnaws [his] present self." Thus, in this and other poems, poetry becomes a purging fire of sorts for Walker. Clearing and cleaning the mind's own thickets with "Tendrils of flame," the poem establishes a space for new life, new growth, to flourish.

In addition to gardens we find a fascination with the coastland of Walker's native Sussex, particularly so in the earlier poetry. In this ambiguous "no-man's land" ("Lancing Beach") of estuaries, salt marshes, mudflats, shorelines, and beaches—not to mention the flora and fauna inhabiting them—Walker finds a briny, brackish liminal space that allows him to ruminate on the human world and its delicately complex relations with the natural world. As he tells Wilmer:

I try to use animals for their human references, but I'm very interested in natural history, so if the poem exists on two levels that's alright by me. Now Ted Hughes goes more to the essence of the creature than I do, to the wildness of the thing. When he describes a flower you feel the world's about to end. I deal with wildness too, but it's the delicacy of a thing that strikes me as the most important aspect. I go for that.[xvi]

If Hughes goes to "the wildness" and "essence of the creature" then Walker goes to the creaturely essence of the human. He does this particularly well in the poem "Grebe" from *Fox on a Barn Door*. Observing what is a common sight on Sussex waterways, a Great Crested Grebe "using the water like land," the speaker is prompted to reflect on his own mutability:

> I can forget the mammal
> that I am for days; and though
> in the womb I was reptile,
> fish, I have no memory
> of the scales I shed, and no
> sense of the gekko in me.
>
> But you—are you going back
> to be again what once you were
> before your ancestors shook
> their first wet feathers and flew
> into the alien air
> you find so alien now?

From these stanzas we can see how "Grebe" is both poignant and humorous. On the one hand, Walker indulges in a number of irresistible puns, implying, for instance, that the poem's speaker has the memory of a gold fish: "fish, I have no memory." But the "scales" this fishy poet sheds, are not only those of his aquatic ancestors but also the reptilian, snake-like, scales of his Adamic provenance. Additionally, these scales are also those comprising what pre-Darwinian scientists called "the Great Scale of Being" (*Scala Naturae*). This pre-evolutionary concept proposed a fixed hierarchical chain of being that regards humanity as the pinnacle of creation. The poem clearly counters such a viewpoint by suggesting that both grebe and human have evolved from fish and can, contrary to the *fixed* chain of being, "be again what [they] once were."

Human sovereignty is further undermined in "Grebe" when the poem's speaker confesses that he has "no / sense of the gekko in me." We might wonder why Walker chooses "gekko" instead of the more generic "lizard." Undoubtedly, one reason is that it sounds good. Indeed, it is a wonderfully odd and incongruous phrase both in terms of sound, spelling, and reference and is another instance of Walker delighting in the very physical qualities of language. But it is also worth noting that this species of lizard, which Walker would have seen in abundance when he first visited Spain as a teenager, is largely nocturnal. Whereas humans have evolved over millennia in response to the stimulating and nourishing effects of the sun and taken that solar power as the figurative or symbolic ideal of rational, enlightened intellect—the light of reason—these lizards possess a different but equally valid kind of "sense" that humans have lost.

Indeed, in "Grebe" Walker makes some important claims about human kinship with the natural world. In losing touch with our environment and experiencing it as something "alien" or "other," the poem implies, we are also losing touch with something of ourselves: in no longer making "sense" of our world, how can we "make sense" of ourselves? By shedding our prescribed ideas about what it is that makes or defines us as human—and the often damaging values that accrue with such ideas—we can experience and value our environment in new ways. It is this aspect of Walker's work that Vernon Young singles out and lauds. Reflecting on Walker's relative neglect in his review of *Gloves to the Hangman* for *The Hudson Review,* Young asserts that:

> No poet writing in England today has a closer, more recondite knowledge of the secret life in the non-human universe than Ted Walker. In each of his four volumes to date, mystifyingly ignored by the poets and professors who compile our anthologies, Walker has been contriving quiet, hair-raising (and musically precise) metaphors from his great gift for relating our inattentive senses to the cryptic features of animals, fish, birds—flowers, even—in which, if we paused to look (with *his* patience and his occult powers) we would see ourselves, or the wreck of our selves, writ plain.[xvii]

Using animals and their environs as a way of articulating human concerns means that Walker's poetry often avoids the confessional tone of other poets he admires, particularly Robert Lowell and Sylvia Plath.[xviii] Throughout Walker's work, the natural world comes to speak on behalf of the psychological complexities of human life. Landscape becomes the trigger for recalling significant memories, experiences, and for addressing the fraught tensions of domestic and family life. Often, we are presented with an image of the solitary poet alone with his thoughts in the landscape, as in "Easter Poem"—from which *Fox on a Barn Door* takes its title—where the poet has "gone on Easter Day / early and alone to be / beyond insidious bells / (that any other Sunday / I'd not hear) up to the hills."[xix] In poems such as these it is hard not to recall the "lofty thoughts" and solitary reflections of Wordsworth, as the poem's speaker becomes a fellow "worshipper of Nature" and, like Wordsworth before him, finds in it "the anchor of [his] purest thoughts" and "soul / Of all [his] moral being."[xx]

In Walker's poetry, however, the purest thoughts nursed by nature are more often than not melancholy and pensive rather than sublime and elevated. In "Starlings," for example, this commonplace bird, flocking "high in the misproportioned limbs / of our imaginings," becomes the shadowy augur of our deepest, intangible fears and menacing uncertainties. Likewise, in "The Night Bathers" a solitary excursion in Cardiganshire, Wales moves the poem's speaker to acknowledge "Remorse" about his frustrated relationship with his son which, in turn, prompts memories about the poet's own relationship with his father. "I see," he writes,

> by astonishing bonfires
> in an idleness of yachts
> my father running down the beach
> twenty grown years ago, at home;
>
> when he was young to understand
> why, momently out of the night

and purposeful beyond the reach
of all his worry, I had swum
deep into banks of sea-fret
too far to have to answer him.

As "The Night Bathers" suggests, it is not just nature's seasons and rhythms that are cyclical but family dynamics too. With parenthood, Walker implies, comes the realisation that other, familial, patterns of behaviour and repetition can occur that are all too easily as inevitable as the causality of the seasons. Although this doesn't necessarily mean that Walker, like Philip Larkin, is claiming that, "Man hands on misery to man" and families "fuck you up," his poetry does, on occasion, express a need to escape from the domestic sphere.[xxi] This is apparent in "Hothouse" where Walker invokes a place in the mind "where the man could be alone / from choice, free from his children / and not at home to his friend; / where husband was husbandman." But for all these desires for freedom from domestic and social duty, Walker is ultimately a poet of the hearth; that locus of warmth, stability and place of family convergence. It is the thing that Walker always returns to in his poetry. Although Walker's poetry often shows a desire to burn the English ivy of his own sensibilities and escape to non-domestic, foreign fields—both in his translations of various European poets and physical travels to Spain and Australia that he writes about in *Mangoes on the Moon*—there is always the counter pull of the hearth, "the place," Walker writes in "One Magpie for Sorrow," "where I belong."

The tension between his family responsibilities and his literary vocation is something that Walker spent his career attempting to reconcile and negotiate. In 1966, Walker was co-winner, with Stevie Smith, of the Cholmondeley Award for Poets. Writing to the Award's patron, Sybil, Marchioness of Cholmondeley (who would become a lifelong friend of Walker's) he explains the impossible compromise of being a good father and a dedicated poet.[xxii] Walker was fortunate to have a number of opportunities to devote time and energy to his writing. One significant opportunity presented itself in 1979 when Walker was awarded a travel scholarship of £750 by the Society of Authors to live for three months—from May 16th to August 14th—in Cuenca, Spain. The reason for the trip was to write, which Walker evidently did. However, the trip also gave him the opportunity to reflect on, and take stock of, his life and career. In a letter to his friend and fellow poet, John Ormond, Walker expresses the hope that upon his return from Cuenca he will be a different man.[xxiii] This introspective soul-searching gave him the incentive for writing new poems that address his relationship with his wife Lorna. In a letter to Ormond, Walker writes of his plans for a book of poems, dedicated to Lorna, entitled "Love Songs from Castille" [sic], which will declare in verse the depth of love he felt for Lorna and the sanctity of a relationship he felt he had too easily taken for granted.[xxiv]

A small number of the poems that Walker wrote on his Cuenca trip were published later, and after considerable revision, in his final collection, *Mangoes on the Moon*. As well as something of a play on words ("man goes on the moon")— something that Walker takes delight in throughout his poetry—the title of this, Walker's last collection, is also a reference to Philip Larkin's assertion that, "The notion of expressing sentiments in short lines having similar sounds at their ends seems as remote as mangoes on the moon."[xxv] Larkin is a considerable influence on Walker's later poetry and largely supersedes the earlier influence of Hughes, as Walker becomes increasingly preoccupied with a similar kind of England that Larkin presents in his understated and matter-of-fact way. And when Walker is distanced from his country of birth (as well as Spain, *Mangoes on the Moon* also records Walker's time Australia) the pull toward it and the family memories it embodies becomes all the more vehement.

A number of the Cuenca poems have remained, until now, unpublished. "Celibate," "Above Cuenca," and "Hierbas Buenas" in the present selection are all taken from Walker's correspondence to Ormond, which is held in the Ted Walker archive at the University of Chichester library. This material provides penetrating insight into Walker's literary and personal life. Walker, it quickly emerges, was a gifted writer of letters. His letters to John Ormond and Sybil, Marchioness of Cholmondeley are warm, affectionate, humorous affairs that show a man in love equally with the written word and his family. Warm exchanges from notable literary figures including Ted Hughes, Sir John Betjeman, Robert Lowell, Laurie Lee, and Leslie Norris are held in the archive and indicate the extent of Walker's gregarious and personable nature, as well as his enthusiastic and engaged involvement with the wider literary world.

It remains to consider why Walker's poetry has fallen into relative neglect and why it merits re-discovering and re-reading now. Looking at the review clippings that Walker collected (and which can be consulted in the Ted Walker archive at Chichester), it is apparent that the interest, enthusiasm, and praise bestowed on *The Fox on a Barn Door* waned considerably with each successive publication. Ian Hamilton's rather unforgiving review of Walker's sophomore effort, *The Solitaries*, is a harsh indicator of the reception to be given the work that followed *Fox on a Barn Door*:

> Ted Walker's second book is a serious disappointment in the sense that it gives full licence to the faults that marred the promise of his first. His eye for fierce natural detail is still steady and specific but he seems much less interested in images than in convincing us that he can think. Ponderous and prosy, and at the same time full of his own significance, he falters into the feebly sermonising.[xxvi]

To a degree, Walker was the victim of his own success. No doubt, as a consequence of his early achievement he felt a certain amount of pressure to live up to the reputation that he had secured himself with *Fox on a Barn Door*. Unfortunately, as Jeremy Robson astutely writes in *The Tribune*, "Over-praise for an unusually promising first volume has given way to under-praise for an accomplished follow-up."[xxvii] Sympathetic readers, such as the poet Norman Nicholson, did see Walker meeting, even exceeding, such high expectations. Writing in the *Church Times*, Nicholson claims that, "*The Solitaries* fulfils all the promise of 'Fox on a Barn Door' [sic] and shows clear signs of development."[xxviii] However, most reviewers sharing Hamilton's sentiments found that Walker's "nature" poetry was too limited in its scope. Terry Eagleton's review of *The Night Bathers* is a good example of this. The noted Marxist critic stresses Walker's need to extend his "delicate complexity of [...] feel for the natural world," and "sensitivity into a fuller engagement with moral situations."[xxix] According to Eagleton:

> Walker's poems aren't, as yet, morally *interpretative*, in the sense of reflecting significantly on the richness they record. They hesitate in explicitly relating what they say of the world to complex states of human feeling, leaving their overall attitudes hinted, half-implicit.[xxx]

Walker, it would appear, heeded such criticisms and reservations about his work. In later collections he ventures into translating the work of a number of European poets, including Paul Verlaine, Pablo Neruda, Rainer Maria Rilke, Salvatore Quasimodo, and Frederico Garcia Lorca. He explains in a brief prefatory note to *The Night Bathers* that his translations "seem to provide a continuity of theme or mood" with his own poems.[xxxi] They also significantly amplify Walker's own poems, broaden their scope, and overcome their limitations and restrictions. In short, these translations— such as Paul Verlaine's "Sunsets" and "O My Gentle Creatures" by Salvatore Quasimodo, which are included in the present volume —provide Walker an opportunity for stepping beyond his own limiting subjectivity as well as enable him to write in a more detached and impartial voice. "The main reason he does so much translating," Clive James conjectures, "is probably that his own poems are limited, as well as fuelled, by his extraordinary penetration of nature, and the seed-catalogue specificity of terminology that seems to go with the cast of mind."[xxxii] According to James:

> From the make-up of this collection [*The Night Bathers*] it's permissible to assume that Mr. Walker has sensed his danger and consequently stiffened his own work with translations of poems which attempt and achieve a greater amplitude of utterance — poems which may start out from nature but which get something said without being dragged down into the concrete detail of chaffinch-husks and the precise pitch of a bloodwort's warble.[xxxiii]

Another notable venture of Walker's is his children's poetry. Walker provided the poetry for *The Lion's Cavalcade*, a beautifully illustrated book by Alan Aldridge that Jonathan Cape published in 1980. The book was based on the poem *The Lion's Masquerade and Elephant's Champêtre*, penned anonymously by "A Lady" in 1808. Because Walker's verse establishes such an enchanting dialogue with Aldridge's illustrations, it was decided that to simply reproduce his text *sans* image, in the present volume, would not do justice to the poem. What is represented in this volume, however, is *Grandad's Seagulls*. Published in 1994 by Blackie Children's Books, this collection of children's poems pertinently parallels Walker's adult work. In it we find poems about familiar avian subjects such as rooks and blackbirds, and, in "Goldfish in the Garden Pond," Walker presents what is probably the closest he has ever come to writing haiku:

> Basking close to the sun as they are able,
> They turn the afternoon into a fable:
> Spillings of rich coins on a miser's table.

Walker's laconic use of words presents a vivid image as he puns on the priceless pleasures that the *gold*fish afford the observer. But for all its wit and light-heartedness, this children's poem could comfortably be included in one of Walker's adult collections. Indeed, what is particularly notable about *Grandad's Seagulls* is the way that typical characteristics and topics of Walker's poetry are discernable throughout the collection. In "Awake" there is a level of anxiety, unease, and sense of mutability that recalls early poems such as "Starlings" and "Breakwaters." Also, the apostrophising in "An Old Rook" and "Blackbird," as well as the sentient ambience of the night in "Awake," are further instances of Walker deftly anthropomorphising his non-human subjects, making them breathe, speak, stir, and act in ways that imbue them with an irresistible level of familiarity and intimacy.

An abiding strength of Walker's poetry is its uncanny ability to reveal and disclose the familiar in new, transformative and revelatory light. Be it the Sussex coast, flora and fauna, family life, or the fragility of human relationships, Walker addresses these, and other themes, in fresh, often unnerving, ways. For, as much as it celebrates the manifold affections of the heart, Walker's poetry shows no qualms in confronting that more difficult subject: the heart's afflictions. Indeed, what emerges from this new selection of Walker's poetry is the sense of a poet passionately devoted to his art. Walker was, in all sense of the word, committed to poetry. To the best of his abilities, and as much as his circumstances permitted, he adhered to the demanding sentence the craft demands. Thus, Richard Holmes's belief that, "There is something inescapably occasional about [Walker's] writing, something of the Sunday painter" requires correction.[xxxiv] Indeed, a letter from Leslie Norris to Walker, now in the Walker Archive at Chichester, paints a much more accurate picture of Walker's achievements. In his letter, Norris compares Walker to Seamus Heaney, believing that his work was on a par with Heaney's; if not, better. Why Walker never experienced the acclaim and success of Heaney is, Norris believes, due to circumstances. Had a more influential imprint such as Faber published Walker, and had he not had the pressures of teaching, family, and money to contend with, then, Norris believes Walker's career could have taken a different turn. Norris concludes his insightful reflections by reassuring Walker that when the time comes for the publication of his "Collected Poems" he will finally get the recognition he deserves. For, as Norris stresses, Walker never was a second division player.[xxxv]

Norris's comments are a poignant reminder that poetic reputation rests, ultimately, on more than just skill. Walker *had* that in abundance. "Hughes, Larkin, Redgrove. They're good. Are they this good?" Vernon Young writes in his review of *Gloves to the Hangman*.[xxxvi] What Walker did not possess so readily was the opportunity, luck, and financial security so crucial for a poet. We may have to wait a while longer for the "Collected" Walker to emerge but, until that time, it is hoped that this selected edition of what we consider some of Walker's best and most timely work will secure his reputation as a talented and significant poet in the rich and complex currents of post-war British poetry.

Ross Hair,
Department of English & Creative Writing,
University of Chichester, August 2010

---

[i] P. N. Furbank, review of *Fox on a Barn Door*, *The Listener* (July 15, 1965), 101. Ian Hamilton, "Flowers and Porpoises," *The Spectator* (August 13, 1964), n.p. Press clippings from The Ted Walker, University of Chichester.

[ii] A. Alvarez, review of *Fox on a Barn Door*, *The Observer* (June 27, 1965), n.p. Press clippings from The Ted Walker Archive, University of Chichester.

[iii] M. L. Rosenthal, review of *Fox on a Barn Door*, *The New York Times Book Review* (November 20, 1966), 60. Press clipping from The Ted Walker Archive, University of Chichester.

[iv] John Press, "Three New Poets: Ted Walker, Seamus Heaney, Kenneth White," *The Southern Review* 5 (Summer, 1969), 677-78.

[v] For more current examples of Sussex poetry see the recent anthology *A Track of Light: Poetry Inspired by Chichester and West Sussex*, edited by Dave Swann (Chichester: University of Chichester, 2010).

[vi] Walker fondly recounts his memories of Uncle Jack in his autobiography, *The High Path*, and describes the tragic accident that killed him. See Ted Walker, *The High Path* (London, Melbourne and Henley: Routledge & Kegan Paul, 1982), 64.

[vii] Ted Walker interview with Clive Wilmer, *Varsity* 6 (November, 1965), 13. The Ted Walker Archive, University of Chichester Press.

[viii] Ian Hamilton, *The Observer Magazine* (September 23, 1973), 67. Press clipping from The Ted

Walker Archive, University of Chichester.

[ix] Rosenthal, *The New York Times Book Review*, 60. Press clipping from The Ted Walker Archive, University of Chichester.

[x] Ted Walker, *The Solitaries* (London: Jonathan Cape, 1969), 20.

[xi] Donald Davie, *With the Grain: Essays on Thomas Hardy and Modern British Poetry*, ed. Clive Wilmer (Manchester: Carcanet Press, 1998), 3.

[xii] Ibid., 4.

[xiii] Martin Seymour Smith, *The Scotsman* (April 22, 1967), n.p. Press clipping from The Ted Walker Archive, University of Chichester.

[xiv] Peter Porter, "Durrell in Decline," *The Observer* (June 17, 1973), 33. Press clipping from The Ted Walker Archive, University of Chichester.

[xv] Walker, *The High Path*, 158.

[xvi] Walker interview with Clive Wilmer, 13.

[xvii] Vernon Young, review of *Gloves to the Hangman*, *The Hudson Review*, 28. 4 (Winter 1975-76), 599. Press clipping from The Ted Walker Archive, University of Chichester.

[xviii] Plath is one of the poets that Walker can be heard discussing in *Recent Poetry*, an audio recording of his talk about several contemporary poets that interest him who, in addition to Plath, include Hughes, Thom Gunn, Philip Larkin, and Vernon Scannell. Ted Walker, *Recent Poetry*. Cassette recording (London: Sussex Publications, 1982).

[xix] Walker describes, in considerable detail, the provenance and writing of "Easter Poem" in an insightful essay entitled "Writing Poetry," included in *English Poetry*, ed. Alan Sinfield (London: Sussex Books, 1976), 229-39.

[xx] William Wordsworth, "Lines Written a Few Miles Above Tintern Abbey," *The Major Works*, ed. Stephen Gill (Oxford and New York: Oxford World's Classics, 2000), 134-35.

[xxi] Philip Larkin, "This Be Verse," Collected Poems, ed. Anthony Thwaite (London: Marvell and Faber and Faber, 1990), 180.

[xxii] See Ted Walker to Sybil, Marchioness of Cholmondeley, November 7, 1966. The Ted Walker Archive, University of Chichester.

[xxiii] See Ted Walker to John Ormond, May 16, 1979. The Ted Walker Archive, University of Chichester.

[xxiv] See Ted Walker to John Ormond, June 2, 1979. The Ted Walker Archive, University of Chichester.

[xxv] Philip Larkin, *Selected Letters 1940-1985*, ed. Anthony Thwaite (London: Faber and Faber, 1999), 197.

[xxvi] Ian Hamilton, "On the Rhythmic Run," *The Observer* (March 26, 1967), n.p. Press clipping from The Ted Walker Archive, University of Chichester.

[xxvii] Jeremy Robson, review of *The Solitaries*, *The Tribune* (April 21, 1967), n.p. Press clipping from The Ted Walker Archive, University of Chichester.

[xxviii] Norman Nicholson, review of *The Solitaries*, *The Church Times* (August 11, 1967), 6. Press clipping from The Ted Walker Archive, University of Chichester.

[xxix] Terry Eagleton, review of *The Night Bathers*, *The Observer* (April 5, 1970), n.p. Press clipping from The Ted Walker Archive, University of Chichester.

[xxx] Ibid.

[xxxi] Ted Walker, *The Night Bathers: Poems 1966-8* (London: Jonathan Cape, 1970), 7.

[xxxii] Clive James, *The Metropolitan Critic*, (London: Faber and Faber, 1974), 117-18.

[xxxiii] Ibid., 118.

[xxxiv] Richard Holmes, review of *The Night Bathers*, *The Times* (May 2, 1970), n.p. Press clipping from The Ted Walker Archive, University of Chichester.

[xxxv] See Leslie Norris to Ted Walker, February 14, 1996. The Ted Walker Archive, University of Chichester

[xxxvi] Young, *The Hudson Review*, 599. The Ted Walker Archive, University of Chichester.

'The Other Ted': A Biographical Introduction

by Diana Barsham

In an age of celebrity, the old notion that poets should be known only for the quality of their poems is not one that, in the end, serves poetry well. Though it may try to create one, poetry does not exist in a vacuum; it is shaped by, and subject to, the same cultural forces that can make a well-written Life powerfully representative of some common quandary or aspiration. The best-known poets of the post-war period, Philip Larkin, Ted Hughes and Sylvia Plath, have all had their reputations consolidated and expanded by the work of biographers for, as Dr. Johnson recognised, the lives of poets possess a special cultural resonance. Paula R. Backscheider offers one explanation for this when she argues: "writers are believed to have secret, creative, even fantasy-rich imaginations" which "seem to offer unusual opportunities to understand the interior, subjective life"[i]. In the case of Ted Walker, the most important and distinctive features of his writing are illuminated by setting them within that framework of inner and outer events which shaped his career.

Like other poets of the two post-war generations, Ted Walker was involved in the struggle to recast the enduring legacy of English Romanticism, particularly that nature poetry associated with the pastoral tradition, in relation to the changed subjectivities of twentieth-century democracy. For Walker, the wrestle with Romanticism was part of his response to that crisis of post-war masculinity which D.H. Lawrence had, after World War One, already identified with the English class system. "I was", Walker writes, "entangled in Romanticism like a sapling wrapped round with ivy... Gradually, however, I began to tell the sham from the true"[ii]. A writer averse to the American vogue for confessional poetry, he evolved instead a poetic idiom which not only dramatised "a man speaking" [iii]but also, and more unusually, invoked a dialogic context, full of diverse but intimate interlocutors. In an age of BBC poetry broadcasts, Walker's good linguist's ear inclined him always to regard poetry as a mode of dialogue. As an adolescent, he had been an avid writer of fan letters to men he admired like T.S. Eliot or the Dali Lama, and the impulse to use both his poems and his translations to bridge cultural and personal distances was one he never lost. In *After the funeral*, he addresses his old friend, William Plomer, who died in 1973:

> It is hard, thinking of you as dead,
> *You* now dumb. For the first time it is you not I
> Who owe letters. I'll have, somehow, to do without
> Your old-fashioned and unphonable presence who
> Could be written to nights, mornings of blank despair
>
> When no voice may be heard bearably answering back. [iv]

Walker's characteristic use of poetic waterscapes reinforces this gift for communicating across difficult emotional depths. "Bridges", he claimed, "are rare over still water".[v] In his satirical *Letter to Marcel Proust,* a self-confessed working class yob ("Semites I loathed, and next to Semites, queers") gaily talks himself into alignment with the high culture of a Jewish homosexual.[vi]

Walker's conflicted self-awareness and his careful self-positioning are tactical weapons in his wrestle with Romanticism. His subjectivity nurtured by the English nature tradition, a poet who, as Clive James recognised, "knew his way round a garden"[vii], Walker was also aware that the egalitarian political perspectives associated with the work of Wordsworth, Clare, Cobbett and Hardy had reached a climax of achievement. Like Larkin, his poems often revisit issues unresolved in the work of his forbears, including the perennially uncomfortable housing of creative solitude within the bosom of the family:

> guiltily I stop with less
> than ten miles to go
> and dial my number. My voice
> seems confident as it says,
>
> *it's good to be coming home,*
> *looking forward to seeing you,*
> having a practised cadence,
> habitual, therefore true.
> And as the last turnings come
> through the hanger wood, I sense
>
> a relief in familiar
> landscapes of a solitude
> rooted here.
> (Journey Back)[viii]

This issue in particular confronted him in the late 1970s when a travel grant from the Society of Authors offered him the prospect of three months writing in Spain away from family responsibilities:

> For anyone born in my particular narrow band of the class spectrum – of an artisan, Puritan, Protestant Work Ethic, Band of Hope, Co-Operative Wholesale Society, Left Book Club, Pledge-signing, Paying on the Nail, Fabian, Complete Works of Dickens, and Sunday School background – a husband leaving home to pursue his own selfish ends would have merited...a banshee choir of local disapprovers.

> But I was going, and that was that. [ix]

As Ross Hair convincingly argues in his critical introduction, it is impossible to read Walker for long and still question his significance for British poetry. Like his more famous contemporaries, Walker tackles two of the big topics in post-war British culture: the impact of gender redefinitions on family life and the changing environmental consciousness of human and animal spiritualities. Where the conservative Larkin came to represent a fastidious, solitary selfhood on the side of the animals, Plath and Hughes quickly became established as iconic carnivores in the tragic mythology of monogamous marriage. A complex hybrid of the "cushy south", a Midlands working class family background and a grammar school, Oxbridge education, Walker's identity is in many ways a reverse image of the poet with whom he was so often compared, Ted Hughes.

If Walker was restricted as a man by the collective consciousness of his class, as a poet he had a long arm, a reach far beyond the grasp of others. Significantly, the one sport at which he excelled was throwing the discus, an activity suited to his heavy build and his resistance to the schoolboy ethos of *team spirit* but metaphorically expressive of his poetic powers:

> The action is one of the most beautiful movements in sport. Performing it perfectly is deeply satisfying. All the muscles from toes to fingertips have to be precisely co-ordinated. The small throwing circle imposes a stringent discipline. From stillness, within a bare second, the thrower uncoils to attain maximum acceleration. Strength and speed – controlled – engender grace.[x]

Walker always took pleasure in watching closely "whatever was in motion, fast or slow", determined to master the art of making his poems "catch the movement" of what he observed"[xi]. Poetry was a projectile art. He learnt this at school while trying to comfort his weeping French master recently rejected by a girl friend. When Walker suggested the girl might return, the teacher wailed in frustration: "There's a million other girls...but only one copy of the sonnet sequence I threw in her window as that train steamed out of Grimsby"[xii].

    With Ted Walker's death still recent - he died in 2004 - one reason, perhaps, why no biography of him has yet appeared is due to his own success as a life-writer. Walker's first volume of autobiography, *The High Path*, dedicated to his family "Present, Past and Future", provides an account of his war-time childhood, his meeting with Lorna Benfell, the beautiful girl who was to become his first wife, and his departure for Cambridge in 1953. Written in Spain in 1979 as Lorna began her long battle with the cancer that eventually killed her, **The High Path** won the J.R. Ackerley Prize for autobiography on its publication in 1982. Its sequel, *The Last of England*, serialised on Radio 4, was published ten years later in 1992 and dedicated to his grandchildren. Set in 1987, the year of Lorna's death, it tells in devastating detail the story of her fatal illness, the impact of his own bereavement and his determination to make a life for himself beyond it. His remarkable travel narrative, **In Spain**, also appeared in that life-changing year, 1987. Written to celebrate the country he came to regard as his spiritual home, it invokes a period when his life, rather than his poetry, carried the centrifugal force of the thrown discus.

    These works of poetic autobiography make no attempt to provide a chronology of Walker's professional life as teacher, journalist, dramatist, broadcaster and editor. They aim instead to extract "the clear essence of truth from turbid bucketsful dredged from the well of recollection"[xiii], an essence he locates in the precise shade of his wife's eyes, "clear blue as a Chalk Hill butterfly"[xiv]. Meeting her at the age of fourteen and proposing a year later, Lorna became the muse and encourager of Walker's talent: "Whenever I was with Lorna, my perception of the world around us became sharper".[xv] After thirty years of marriage, the climactic moment of his life account occurs when Lorna is told her cancer has spread and that she must lose her right eye. Walker writes: "Words are my trade. I graduated as a linguist. I have taught myself the disciplines of verse and prose and the drama. But there was nothing I knew how to say at that moment" [xvi]. The truth was deserting him; for over a decade his poetry was to do the same. Failing to persuade Lorna to wear a black eye patch instead a replacement optic, he found himself mesmerised by that "fake eye, with its steadfast, terrifying, penetrating gaze". [xvii] The sign under which much autobiography is written, this image of the false eye provides an ironic twist to Walker's writing career. Where Wordsworth's autobiography, **The Prelude**, (1804, 1850) had provided a sublime account of the growth of a poet's mind and the discovery of his vocation, Walker's charted instead its decline and disappearance.

The external facts of Walker's life are easily available, part of a new, distinctly post-war demographic. Born on the 28th of November 1934, he was the son of a West Midland's carpenter who had married and come south in search of work, settling in a small block of flats on the Lower Brighton Road between Lancing and Shoreham. Other close relatives soon migrated south to join him, creating an extended family in adjoining flats overlooking the saltwater lagoon known as 'Widewater' just inland of Lancing beach. To the north lay the Adur Valley and the expansive beauty of the South Downs.

Walker's intelligence and his family's self-sacrificing aspirations won him first a place at Steyning Grammar School and then at St John's College, Cambridge, where he read Modern Languages. In 1956, straight after graduation, he married Lorna Benfell at St Mary de Haura Church in Shoreham. While working as a teacher, first in London and later in Bognor Regis and Chichester, Walker set up and edited a poetry magazine, **Priapus**, with his colleague, John Cotton. His first pamphlet of poems, rather ominously entitled **Those Other Growths**, was published in 1964 when Walker was thirty. The early 1960s brought him immediate success as one of the new generation of Cambridge poets. His first book, **Fox on a Barn Door**, (1965) won him both the Eric Gregory and the first ever Cholmondeley Award (1966); his second, **The Solitaries**, (1967) attracted the Alice Hunt Bartlett Prize. Three further volumes appeared in the 1970s: **The Night Bathers** (1970) was followed by **Gloves to the Hangman** (1973) whose title poem is a brilliant dramatic monologue by the fourteenth century French farmer who brutally executed a pig, following its trial for the murder of a small child. Walker was elected a Fellow of the Royal Society of Literature in 1975 and, in 1978, published **Burning the Ivy,** his last volume of poems before Lorna was diagnosed with cancer and the muse deserted him.

Established as a significant British poet, the distinctly Europhile Walker became a Professor of Creative Writing at the Sussex campus of an American University, the New Hampshire College of Concord. Colleagues recall him as a strong, flamboyant, likeable character, a dramatic presence in the classroom; Walker himself found teaching a serious drain on his creative resources. Following their return to West Sussex, he and Lorna bought a house in the village of Eastergate which they named "Breakwaters" after one of his early poems. An old agricultural village with an ancient tithe barn, the Wilkes Head pub, and its church in a farm yard, Eastergate intersects sharply with the modern world via a busy stretch of the A 29, the main road to Bognor Regis.

As autobiography invariably owes its interpretative stance more to the time from which it is written than from any unchanging chronological truth, the date of 1979 when Walker began work on **The High Path** is an important one. Away from home on his travel bursary to Spain, Walker stood on the threshold of a personal and political crisis. With Margaret Thatcher's government in power and decisive battle with the TUC immanent, it was no longer possible to believe or find inspiration in that version of England which had delivered Old Labour style politics in a green-sleeved dress of folklore and nostalgia. In university English Departments throughout the country, D. H. Lawrence and Thomas Hardy were being replaced on the curriculum by Feminism and Literary Theory. As Lorna's illness became synchronised with a right-wing revolution, Walker found himself an early convert to Feminism. It would, he argued, help to remove "the oppressively heavy moral obligation on husbands and fathers to be the ultimately responsible bread winners and strong, protective, ever-present arms"[xviii].

It was at this point that Walker began to write his elegy for the working class childhood that had so decisively shaped his masculinity to fit the mould of 'the family man'. As he wrote, the suppressed contents of his poetry, its haunting ambivalent imagery, began to unpack itself in prose. It had always been Walker's habit to write down first a factual, detailed description of what he'd seen, including small as well as large details. This descriptive picture would then, by what he called 'accident', release a resonant image from "the hard, concrete, factual detail". These 'accidents' were the core of Walker's poetic technique, flooding his stanzas with evocative, often Christianised, references. Not for nothing was Walker the son of a carpenter and a mother called Mary, who woke from their wedding night to find it was Christmas morning.

This poetic apprenticeship served Walker well as an autobiographer. Growing up in the construction industry, his memory was saturated with material. Re-assembling the details of an asthmatic, humdrum childhood on the Lower Brighton Road, he creates a sense of special privilege for himself though his first hand knowledge of textures and surfaces of every kind. Coal, sand, water, wood and rock speak to him in a plethora of tongues. Waking at first light, his pleasure as a child was to fingernail sand from the crevices in his own body. He recalls his instinct for "the sensual and onomatopoeic gut-naming" of proximate, familiar things, "the freshly minted syllables betokening our bodies' response to the look and feel and taste and smell of the lovely stuffs of our paradise"[xix]. Offered the consolations of a sand pit on his traumatic first day at school, he rejected the synthetic yellow stuff inside it as an insult to truth.

As with Keats, sensual awareness generated the imagery of his poems, especially his childhood encounters with the fascinating substances of the beach: the slippery touch of eel grass, the sharp edge of muscle shells against his legs, the popping, greasily oozing seaweed on stretches of sand formerly sewn with land mines against a German invasion. The textures and surfaces of the human body, in particular, produce in **The High Path** an autobiographical hymn to libidinal inhibition. When nine year old Shirley shows him her bottom and demands a sight of his in return, Walker's path to experience is blocked by 'the baroque complexity' of braces he cannot unfasten. After Shirley, the seeds of sexuality begin to "germinate, sprout and flourish" in "a heavy welter of lush foliage".[xx] Another inspiring 'accident' signals the start of adolescence. During a ball game, his hand accidentally comes into contact with a girl's breast. "Sensuality filled me to the brim, as from a tap turned full on". His imagination takes on the colour of "a riotous Oriental sunrise"[xxi].

Meanwhile, a sense of cultural barriers begins to build up between the grammar school educated son and his working class parents. For his father, Walker's feelings remain particularly intense, full of insight and empathy as he recalls the moment he first asserted independence from him. Shivering on the beach after school, the adolescent boy waits for his father to come and call him in to his homework, then wades out to sea and swims deliberately in the opposite direction.[xxii] This episode appears in the title poem of **The Night Bathers**, demonstrating the ease with which Walker juggled poetry and autobiography across the painful lacunae of father/ son relations. The story of a manhood achieved, **The High Path** concludes as he and his 'prize', the blue eyed Lorna, make their transition into the world of adult experience.

Simultaneously poetic autobiography and detailed historical record, **The High Path** illustrates Walker's belief that the poet is a truthful transmitter of human norms and not an aberration from them. One paranormal strand, however, complicates Walker's sense of identity, that of the double or doppelganger whose presence becomes a feature of his autobiographical writing. The doppelganger manifests itself both as a divided self and as an alternative identity: "I was," Walker observes, "two different boys".[xxiii] One self is macho and violent, especially in male company; the other, tender and solitary, cradling a dead seagull in his arms beyond the gates of the school. Reflecting on the writing of autobiography, Walker invokes this shadow self with that "palimpsest of an alternative existence" that belongs with it:

> My doppelganger flits about between the lines of this book. If I were to ghost write for him, I should begin every sentence with *if only...* Speculation about roads not taken is not necessarily a futile exercise. .. we could at any moment take thought and explore the neglected lanes to previously rejected destinations... I strike a match, murmur that I could have been – still could be –other than I am: the twin brother who catches a different bus of a morning[xxiv] .

Entering the 'lost domain' of his father's childhood on a visit to the Worcestershire village of Shrawley, Walker sees his father cry for the first time, recalling his two brothers both killed in the war. What kind of man, Walker wonders as he contemplates the tombs of his ancestors, might he have become had he grown up in Worcestershire? With his sharp sense of what it means to be an outsider, he reflects on the story of the wicked local lord, who, in penance for his sins, refused to let himself to be buried in consecrated ground.

Like a surprising number of other writers, Walker is haunted too by the ghost of a little sister, Ruth, who died aged only three weeks old. His father could remember seeing the hospital orderly cycling towards the mortuary with the little corpse bundled under his arm like a bag of soiled laundry.[xxv] Highly sensitive to places where the grief of war trauma still lingered, Walker's self definition as a family man includes this connection with lost others and communities of suffering.

The climatic image of **The High Path** refers to another numinous occasion, a peak experience illustrating his "uncommon gift for chancing upon a mystical surprise.[xxvi] Walking alone on the Downs near the prehistoric hill fort of Cissbury Rings, he obeys a sudden instinct to start digging with his sheath-knife at a patch of turf covered with bee-orchids. As his hands bleed freely into the soil, he unearths an ancient grave, digging out first the skull and then the jaw bone of a Bronze Age man. While Walker dozes in the sun after his exertions, the skull itself keeps watch, impassively surveying the cricket match below:

> I saw my skull beside the juniper bush staring from its sockets towards the panorama...In a sense, it *was* my skull I saw: my own skull. There was no smile over the bone...I stared back at him for a long while...When I picked him up, he was warm to the touch.[xxvii].

Walking back to Steyning with the skull under his arm, Walker self-consciously aligns his writing with that of the Romantics when he encounters a local version of Wordsworth's "Idiot Boy" waiting at the bus stop.

This meeting between the living and the dead in a continuity of masculine vision is a pivotal moment in Walker's autobiography, a moment of identity choice. That evening, with Lorna away at Sue Bridehead's training college in Salisbury, Walker sets off for the romance of Brighton, hungry for the adventure of living human bodies. Though he admires the Teddy boys in their flashy outfits, he remains an onlooker, trammelled in different aspirations: "In my blazer and worsted, I was debarred from their dimension of experience". On the train home, he ignores the pert bottom of Eileen Toms and settles down instead to read a newly purchased, second hand book. The die is cast. His evening of excitement ends with a glimpse of his father, mixing his bedtime cocoa through the kitchen window. In the Christmas holidays, Lorna and he leave her brother's wedding early, slipping away to consummate their love in front of a roaring fire: "My manhood established, my curiosity assuaged, I no longer required the frippery delights of Brighton".[xxviii] Secure within a network of family masculinities, this more fortunate Jude the Obscure, "white, male, English, heterosexual and intelligent"[xxix] is finally set to take his place at Oxbridge.

Critics detecting a lack of what Terry Eagleton called "moral interpretation"[xxx] in Walker's nature poetry, have suggested that he turned to translation in order to supply the limitations of his own talent but Walker's predicament was more culturally significant, less individual, than this suggests. The English working class pastoral tradition of Crabbe, Clare and Hardy had, by the 1970s, reached an impasse; it no longer knew what it had left to say. Beyond this, the spiritual and emotional pieties of 'Dover Beach' drifted uneasily along the storm-battered shoreline of the South coast. When critics compared him unfavourably to 'the other Ted', Walker made an important distinction. Hughes, he said, was attracted to the power of wildness, he to its delicacy and vulnerability. Even the wild swans flew towards him through "starved air", their survival hazardous and uncertain. [xxxi]

It was his skill as a linguist that enabled Walker to find a way through the impasse of the 1980s as he watched the England he loved transformed by Thatcherism and his wife disfigured by recurrent cancers:

> Professionally I walked in an empty cul-de-sac; my gift for poetry had long since deserted me, along with the treacherous swallows – and by now I was beginning to accept that it would never come back... I did not have it in mind ever to return to the classroom.[xxxii]

Walker met this crisis by turning to translation, building bridges over troubled water, as his doppelganger began slowly and painfully to reconstruct a new phase of his identity. Between his two volumes of autobiography, Walker wrote his acclaimed travelogue, **In Spain**, begun in 1983 and published 1987, the year of both Lorna's death and the publication of his Selected Poems: **Hands at a Live Fire**.

Spain was to become Walker's salvation, his paradise regained. As a child, his mother had once bought home fifty Spanish oranges from Shoreham market, their golden discs radiant in the gloom of the small family living room. From then on oranges were, for Walker at least, the only fruit. His first visit to Spain had been with his family in 1955, as a Cambridge undergraduate full of "insufferable Oxbridge snobbery"[xxxiii]. He returned a few years later, working as a semi professional courier with a party of Manchester school children inadvertently lodged above a brothel. Tendrils of Spanish flame were woven throughout his upbringing. During the Spanish Civil War, his uncle had wanted to join the International Brigade; his father, a dispatch rider in the Home Guard, had looted an abridged copy of **Don Quixote** from the requisitioned public school that served as their HQ.

Speaking Spanish gave Walker "another identity, another personality":

Learning the Castilian language determined the course of my life, for the acquisition of a second modern language (I was already good at French) turned me into a linguist; and being a linguist was – and still is – a necessary part of one's training as a writer, teacher and traveller.[xxxiv]

In Spain his doppelganger was firmly in the saddle, tilting at proletarian windmills which tried to prescribe what a modern-minded, "family man" was allowed to do. He recognised himself as "still a frankly newish phenomenon":

... uncomfortable and clumsy in the gentleman's world of publishing and the exotic gentilities of the literary Establishment: persons without inherited money to allow them to see the world beyond their own doorsteps, but also having the cultural millstone of domesticity around their necks...If you harboured occasional thoughts of swaggering the nut-strewn roads, and if you voiced those thoughts... you got dubbed a right bastard to be shunned by family, relatives and friends as a moral pariah. Few writers of my acquaintance with origins similar to mine had satisfactorily resolved this essentially English, educated-working-class dilemma without distressing upheavals.[xxxv]

What lends both **In Spain** and **The Last of England** their remarkable resonance is Walker's ability to bend his time frames so that the Spain he explores, both as working class writer and as grief struck widower, is shot through with uncanny reminders and suppressed memories of earlier selves and former visits. The inner journey illuminates the external surroundings, sometimes with dramatic effect. Staying again at the same hotel where he had begun writing **The High Path**, Walker's brief, euphoric sense of freedom after Lorna's death is quickly punctured when he drops his denture in the wash-basin and watches it break in half. Remembering "a similar accident here in 1979", the bizarre coincidence fills him with despair: "In the midst of life, we are in farce."[xxxvi] Felt along the palate, Walker knows that grief has rendered him "ludicrous" again.[xxxvii]

In Spain, Walker turns that gaze of life at death and vice versa to good account in his description of the Olvega sausage factory, illuminating the process by which terrified, squealing pigs are efficiently transformed into highly coloured and spicy chorizo. Travel writing itself can do no more than this. The final leg of his spiritual journey takes him to his 'definitive destination': the ancient pilgrimage site of Santiago de Compostella. Though chance encounters with Spain's magnificent bulls restore his courage, Walker returns to England knowing that the greatest test of his faith is still ahead. Moving backwards in time through searing memories of Lorna's suffering as parts of her face are removed one by one, **The Last of England** (1992) also charts new growths in Walker's personal life and the ripening of a later love. A narrative of transformations, this second volume of autobiography vividly captures the disorientating experience of radical change:

All was in flux in life. Nothing, and no one, could be depended upon to be unchanging. The creatures that had peopled your habituated life metamorphosed in ways too baffling to contemplate, let alone explain ... And the one you had loved as long as you remembered, who could always be counted on to love you back, had become unwontedly absent, and would remain absent, and that was that.[xxxviii]

Transformed by bereavement, knowing himself a diminished person in heart, mind and body, this family man finds himself unable to respond any longer to the ties that bind him either to his family or his country. At this time of maximum solitude, Walker was less alone than he thought. The 1980s and 90s saw an implosion in British family life which, with the death of Princess Diana, threatened the monarchy itself. One man's personal story became a record of that public crisis and the lost poetry of an estranging decade.

Gradually, with the help of his four children, his two sons and two daughters, Walker learned to share his grief and finally to take into account the different, but equally intense, suffering of others. The mending of his damaged relationship with his elder son, Edward, was essential to his own recovery, a task requiring honesty as well as introspection:

> Too often during his growing up I had been overbearing, too quick to crush his intelligence and personality with my own...[xxxix]

Episodes of brutal self-encounter helped to restore the lost truth to Walker's vision as he confronted both his own sensuality and his failures as a husband:

> For much of my life, where women were concerned, had I not sometimes tended to be a rather nasty, predatory, sinister, pot-bellied chap? Shamefully and shamingly I had often adventured, motivated by a vanity more swollen even than my paunch, a tomcat curiosity, and a rumbustious, buccaneering approach to every sensual opportunity life had to offer. [xl]

There is nothing like this in **Birthday Letters**. After a brief romance, Walker returned to England, finding his way back into the family through his new role as a grandfather and his second marriage to a long-standing family friend, Audrey Hicks. **The Last of England** concludes with a wedding kiss and Audrey's decision to enrol as a mature student in the Department of English & Creative Writing at what has now become the University of Chichester where Walker's archive is housed.

After his long silence, Walker eventually, in 1999, published one final collection of poetry, **Mangoes on the Moon** (1999) as he and Audrey moved to Valencia to live out his retirement in Spain. With its "oranges out of Eden" [xli] Spain had finally given him what his war-time childhood lacked: that garden of earthly joys with which the schema of Christian autobiography traditionally begins. Appropriately, this final volume is in two parts: the first containing poems inspired by his travels in Australia; the second, poems addressed to his family, his friends and his love for Spain. Dying in 2004, Walker is buried in the churchyard at Eastergate, on the other side of the church from Lorna. For her grave stone, he had chosen the famous line from Philip Larkin: *What will survive of us is love.* Walker's own memorial, as the poet who charted in prose the painful discontinuities of family life, still remains to be written.

Diana Barsham
Department of English & Creative Writing
University of Chichester
August 2010

[i] Paula R. Backschedider, Reflections on Biography, Oxford University Press (1999), p104

[ii] Ted Walker, The High Path, 1982, reprinted by Slightly Foxed editions in 2010, p184

[iii] See A Reason for Translation, http://www.clivejames.com

[iv] From Burning the Ivy, London, Jonathan Cape, 1978, p 19

[v] Ted Walker: 'Rivers' in Burning the Ivy: London: Jonathan Cape 1987, p30

[vi] In Gloves To the Hangman, London: Jonathan Cope, 1973, p45

[vii] A Reason for Translation: http://www.clivejames.com

[viii] Journey Back from The Night Bathers, Jonathan Cape,1970, p35

[ix] Ted Walker, The Last of England, Phoenix, Orion Books Ltd, London 1992, p18

[x] The High Path, p206

[xi] The High Path, p208

[xii] The high Path, p194

[xiii] The High Path, pp56 -57

[xiv] The High path, p 179

[xv] The High Path, p 195-6

[xvi] The Last of England, p91

[xvii] The Last of England, p97

[xviii] The Last of England, p18

[xix] The High Path, p46

[xx] The High Path, p162

[xxi] The High Path, p 72

[xxii] The High Path, p 164

[xxiii] The High Path, p 98

[xxiv] The High Path, pp119-120

[xxv] The High Path, p19

[xxvi] The High Path, p123

[xxvii] The High Path, p125

[xxviii] The High Path, p221

[xxix] The High Path, p222

[xxx] Terry Eagleton, Review of The Night Bathers in The Observer, 5th April, 1970. Eagleton writes: "Walker's poems aren't, as yet, morally interpretative, in the sense of reflecting significantly on the richness they record. They hesitate in explicitly relating what they say of a world to complex states of human feeling, leaving their overall attitudes hinted, half-implicit".

[xxxi] Sunday Drive to the Beach, in The Night Bathers, p16

[xxxii] The Last of England, p7

[xxxiii] In Spain, London: Secker & Warburg, 1987 p5

[xxxiv] The Last of England, 11, 15

[xxxv] The Last of England, p17

[xxxvi] The Last of England, p21

[xxxvii] The Last of England, p31

[xxxviii] The Last of England, p24

[xxxix] The Last of England, p117

[xl] The Last of England, p99

[xli] The High Path, p66

Minting the Sun

A New Selection of Ted Walker's Poetry

From
Fox on a Barn Door
(Poems 1963-64)

By the Saltings

When the wind is in the thrift
gently, down by the saltings
at dawn when the vapours lift;

and pattering sanderlings
run from you rather than fly
across the sandflat screaming;

before the runnels drain dry
among the sea-lavender
and sun severs sea from sky;

there is time enough, under
any listing low-tide hull
of your choosing, to wonder

at the force of it to pull
you to its shelter, alone
as you are and fearful

as some crab beneath some stone.

Breakwaters

Elms are bad, sinister trees.
Falling, one leaf too many,
they kill small boys in summer,
tripped over by a crow's foot,
bored with the business of leaves.

An uneasiness attends
dead elms – timber for coffins,
ammunition boxes. And
breakwaters. Bolts open sores
of orange rust in their flanks,

and yet there is loveliness.
Ultimate green of eelgrass
soothes with the comfort of hair
all the tiny agonies
that crawl in hidden places

and sing when the tide is low
and death is not imminent,
scrabbling in an eczema
of pink and white barnacles
and mussels of midnight blue.

Terrifying as altars
by night, black, a sea-Stonehenge.
Filigrees of little wracks
dance on them at high water
in a devil-dance. They change.

Their male look lasts a few tides;
when the reek is washed away
and the stubble is shaven,
on a tall September night
the sea will take his new brides.

In his calm he will lap them,
then batter their waists away,
emphasize their Celtic heads.
And when they are old and raddled,
thin, thin as a Belsen arm,

they will stand bare and skinny
and their stringent, hard old hearts
will disregard his knocking.
Dour, malignant to the core,
they will try to outlive him.

Estuary

As the image of the sun
after the blinding moment
lasts on the closed lids violet
an instant, and colour comes
across the tight eye's darkness
though the source of light has gone,

so when I take the low lane
between the fields of barley,
with the slither of a sea-
wind sucking the sun-cracked-husks,
to gaze at the sunken hulks
of ships as they flake at noon

in the lapped inlet, I can
recall that, with the tide-race
of boyhood just begun, once
I ran down the jetty steps,
stubbing up pebbles, and stopped
to stare at a bark broken

in three across the open
mudflat, each part with a mast
still and splintering spars, fast
in banks of sand: and though I
remember the terror my
eyes saw treading the decks on

that bright morning with the wind
light now – the wind that had smashed
that great ship fallen, awash
like driftwood, ribbed in fitful
patches of water – yet still
I would wish to be alone

with the loneliness of then;
and free to make my horrors
walk the boards beyond the shore
at the bidding of my will
only; with the power, as well
as to make, to efface them

by turning to see the men
with bright bandana faces
gladdening the noonday as
they picked up the purple winkles
like scatterings of damsons
with salt dried like bloom on them.

Lancing Beach

An asphaltic sea had lain
with a rash of bladder-wrack
breaking out along its back.

It was a sea-leukaemia
and the sea convulsed with it,
throwing up silver brit

and the body of a man.
Here it was they found him, here,
with little eels in his hair,

and from his unstoppered husk
fluid flowed. Balls of black flies
rolled in the pits of his eyes.

I flung a great pearl of grief
with all my strength at the sea's
apathy. Polycrates

soon had his precious pearl back.
The rings I made would not reach
to break on that other beach:

the grief I cast was for me;
lest I lie dead on this sand.
Lie dead. In this no-man's-land

each stone's a necropolis.
An orthodox death. Absurd
to speak comfortable words.

The grief I cast is for me.
There is a smell of sickness –
I must come to terms with this.

The Burning

The stubble burning began
today, fire tonguing furrows
where lately the rats had run
that now, with pheasant and gull,
skulk among rusting harrows
at field-edge out of the pull

of funnelled winds. With the flames'
peremptory signatures
to the season's ending came
a flaked ash of cirrus wisp
tonight, multiple fractures
of yellow trees, a last wasp

kindled in the hips, berries
that cracked in the red spindles
and a thin wind that carries
yet detonation of jays'
wings as the last light dwindles
below the branch-line of yews.

And in the burning fields now
the images are changing.
Sometimes the fires are a row
of children's sunlit faces,
round, in yellow hair tumbling;
or, as a night breeze rises

on a sudden, a saw edge
surging jagged through the straw,
ripping from hollow to ridge
a whole furlong. Tomorrow
will come plovers and jackdaw
flocks to pick a living through

the desolate acres. Oaks,
leafless, will be as thumb-prints
smudged on the sky; rains will soak
each last, cold cinder away.
A sense of panic, no plants
left to grow, strengthens as clay

sweats, cooling. I would wish
the fires to burn a while more,
fruits not to fall from the bush
a while more, nor I to pass
by, till the slate-shine shives are
cut for the coming of ice.

Grebe

Today the April winds blow
in the tippets of your crest;
the waves are hard beneath you,
as by your will. And you stand
wide-winged like a little Christ
using the water like land.

I can forget the mammal
that I am for days; and though
in the womb I was reptile,
fish, I have no memory
of the scales I shed, and no
sense of the gekko in me.

But you – are you going back
to be again what once you were
before your ancestors shook
their first wet feathers and flew
into the alien air
you find so alien now?

Starlings

Our fears, like starlings, gather
with the dusk. Small particles
they come, innumerable,
flying direct from further
skies of mind only guessed at.
Wheeling they circle us, squat

near. If ever a pair of birds
should strut a sunlit pavement
before us, caught in movement
of the day's concern, we goad
them, approach, put them to flight;
sometimes, even, feed them. But

lodged, untouchable by night,
in the high clerestories
of the stone-still, moon-carved trees
we move among, they will not
be put up at our passing
boldly under their roostings.

Sometimes we can keep away
through the long-lain night. Awake
we may avoid them, though flocks
heave throbbing through our dreams, high
in the misproportioned limbs
of our imaginings.

If we should decide to come
to them, hear their mummeries
mock us when one of them stirs
to ripple through all of them,
sacristan black, we may judge
their strength, though they will not budge

before the day. When they go
they leave uneasy calm, as
they turn as one like louvres
letting the sunlight through.
And only the sense remains
of the black beneath the sheen

and the knowledge that the swift
and silent flight of other
birds, unseen, has passed over
by wings more menacing
yet than those of the known starling.

Easter Poem

I had gone on Easter Day
early and alone to be
beyond insidious bells
(that any other Sunday
I'd not hear) up to the hills
where are winds to blow away

commination. In the frail
first light I saw him, unreal
and sudden through a lifting mist,
a fox on a barn door, nailed
like a coloured plaster Christ
in a Spanish shrine, his tail

coiled round his loins. Sideways
his head hung limply, his ears
snagged with burdock, his dry nose
plugged with black blood. For two days
he'd held the orthodox pose.
The endemic English noise

of Easter Sunday morning
was mixed in the mist swirling
and might have moved his stiff head.
Under the hill the ringing
had begun: and the sun rose red
on the stains of his bleeding.

I walked the length of the day's
obsession. At dusk I was
swallowed by the misted barn,
sucked by the peristalsis
of my fear that he had gone,
leaving nails for souvenirs.

But he was there still. I saw
no sign. He hung as before.
Only the wind had risen
to comb the thorns from his fur.
I left my superstition
stretched on the banging barn door.

From
The Solitaries
(Poems 1964-65)

Heron

He comes down to the shadow
that he has left in the shallow
last night. Imperturbable,
pickerel in their stations
barley shift, invulnerable
with him. His feet know these stones.

There are other ways than this:
there are ways only he knows.
In a rickyard where rats are
he could circle, coil his neck,
and with wings at the trail, thrash straw
and spike what he cared to spike.

And there will happen a time
once more for the cheap, random
kill; for striding dikes in March,
rictus agape, wanton, lewd
with his swagger in some ditch,
randy for the taste of toad.

That is for spring. Lethargy
attends easy victory
now. He would slump on his glut,
lumpish with sloth, his wings
lifting, if they lifted, to a flight
without the rhythms of once.

So, while the painted Carolina
duck squat in sets, like china
on the calico water
of dawn, a thick gaze of sleep
on them, the great grey hoarder
of his want, ravening, keeps

the tensile shadow of neck
in readiness round the rock
under him. And, ignoring
the trees where woodpeckers drum
out his hunger, bides, waiting
for the shoal he knows will come.

Founder

I awoke as rushes hissed,
brushing my dream. The stem
fouled the roots of a fig tree.
A day, a night and a day
went by. Nobody came.
We waited. My runt twin wept.

Then there were fangs at my nape.
I was trailed through fallen figs,
meadow-marsh, and up to stone
that, moonlit, I crawled upon
till she brought him and her dugs:
all the strength I had to sap.

He had to be kept alive
long enough to be of use;
when our foster-mother died
I let the woodpecker feed
him, and the shepherds, sometimes.
He worked; cleared an olive grove,

hewed great stones and trimmed them;
laid them as I commanded.
He leaped my wall – but Romule,
noli, noli, Romule,
he moaned before I murdered
him. I looked over Latium,

alone, and saw above my hills
an eagle rising like a sun
to burn upon Liguria,
Picenum and Calabria,
turn, and glide superbly down
to strut along my city walls.

Birthday Song

With winds that strop on little stones
Beside the water's open throat,
A steel November birthday hones
The rusted scissors of the thought
That I am thirty and that I
Have yet to see somebody die.

Had I but asked, when I was young,
To touch my sister's hardened hand
(That three-week sister with one lung,
Whose life I could not comprehend),
I may have learned to look on death
As a triumph in the fight for breath:

Or if, successive mournings since,
I'd seen a misted mirror clear,
Perhaps my mind could countenance
That life is all we have to fear,
Believing lips set in repose
Suggest far less than I suppose.

For, walking where the river's lip
Is wiped by willows that entwine,
Recalling coffin-slings that slip
Through knuckles knowing more than mine,
I look behind my silent tread
And blink as, level with my head,

My birthday morning mints a sun –
A coin to double-lid an eye
That might, before I'm thirty-one,
Secure the image lastingly
Of how a loved one did not look
Before the last time she awoke.

Moths

When there is a fog they come,
the solitaries, some
who pass your door and then
turn and pass and turn again.

They linger with harm in them
underneath the streetlamp's hum;
criminal with loneliness
they sip the evening yellowness

sifting from the evening windows
still uncurtained. Wish follows
wish across the darkened grass
striped with paths of light from glass

so thinly separating you
from what the watchers want to do.

And so you rise, turn off the light,
hoping that the darkness might
warn off the settling mothmen who
will look for other lamps to fly to:

or, perhaps, you draw the curtain,
sit an hour or two uncertain
whether or not you heard a footstep,
whether or not you heard it stop,

whether you would hear it again
trading softly in your garden.
Else, you leave your house, your room,
its lightened loneliness, and come

to windows lit with solaces
for you, and us, the solitaries.

Elegy for a Trotliner

I remember him. Even then,
when we were boys, he looked too worn
to weather out the season
of those winter afternoons
that rasped away the marram dunes.

He used to bring a ball of sun
to dribble from his fork's curled tines
and rinse away; already, often,
half a moon hung like a husk
from fingers of a tamarisk.

All the shingle, seeping, sang
with lives the sea had left the dusk;
intermittently bell-buoys rang
to smaller swells, more faintly, listing
one by one to breakers basting

them where they lay. Anxious, for
the last of his light was wasting,
he strode the souring foreshore.
Swiftly, before the rip-tide
turned, he dug firm sand that sighed

as he lifted it. He strung his line
of a hundred hooks beyond the braid
of matted wracks by the shine
of phosphor: swifter, snood by snood,
crouching, baited. And when he stood

calf-deep to sink the anchored tag,
there were November floes of cold
incising him, shells in the under-drag
to crampon his tread. It was his way
to walk towards the morning sky

and back by water's withdrawing hem
when there were gulls enough to see by.
Sometimes, walking early, I saw him
fling into a shallow box
the flapping catch he tore from the hooks.

I lie awake, cold nights like this,
and when his memory gently shakes
the moonlight through the frosting glass
to fill my room with gulls, the sound
of him will come as a less than wind:

the barren whistle that he left
blowing across the stones and sand
to a field where the linnets lift
over him. Warm as he is now, deep
in the morning of his sleep.

From
The Night Bathers
(Poems 1966-68)

Sunday Drive to the Beach

I park the car in midwinter sun.
The tailgate flashed open, then the slam
Shut slams from the sea wall. My children,
Forgetting me, lope over the marram
In comic pursuit of their salt-crazed dog.

And so starts another wholesome jag
Of ozone, an afternoon's poking
At jetsam. With empty leash I lag
Through fouled sand. A wind is thwacking
Loose flaps of felt on a summer hut,

But how bland this January, how hot
This boat is, fatigued in its oval weals
Of dead paint. I lie in my overcoat
Alongside, spent as a plank. Those oils
Flow that augur delectable sleep,

Slow under the lids – but I must keep
Awake. I stand, shake off the failed week,
And stumbling among boulders, almost trip.
But barefoot, cantering the sand's wet plaque,
The children remember me, and wave,

And I wave, remembering the live
Ice of a January years ago.
I stab down the stones, into their love,
To tell them how wild swans of the starved air
Flew towards me once from the seaward snow.

Sunsets (after Verlaine)

A sickly dawn
floods the fields
with a sadness drawn
from the setting sun

a sadness to sing
sweetly to my heart
that finds forgetting
in a setting sun

strange dreams these are
like the suns that set
like phantoms scarlet
along some shore

merciless passing
passing merciless
like big suns setting
along some shore

For John Charles Walker, Killed on Shoreham Beach

I don't think you would ever have approved
Of being in a poem. 'Mushty, look,'
I hear your spectre saying, 'keep it dark;
I wouldn't want my mates to get to know.'
But, uncle, how else can I honour you?
Time's gone when I could do the things you did.

At Cambridge I came close to what you were,
Being choked by intellectual simoom;
My most cerebral action there was the soft-
Selling of advert space in Cambridge Left
To the boss of a fish-and-chip saloon.
Literally, I wore the coat you wore –

The jacket of the white alpaca suit
You dared the yobs to jeer on Worthing Prom.
My pals all wondered where I'd nicked it from
And, Brando-esque in leather, named a hand
In Poker after me. Two of a kind
I think we were in the days of that coat.

On pay-days in the shipyard you played Brag
Around an oil-drum with a greasy pack
A week's wages slipped through. You'd borrow back
Enough to stand a round of beer later.
Down The Marlipins they say you were
The sort that got offered a man's last fag.

That was before the war. Sometimes your ghost
Enters my mind, dressed in some comical
Garb; aptly in white, on a bicycle,
Fresh from a battle with lime-bags; or wet
After a fifty-foot plunge for a bet
At midnight in the Adur. It was just

Your luck to get away with it. And when
I get most sick of gentility
And all my life's careful futility –
Pruning the bloody roses for next year,
Setting the prunings tidily on fire,
Sweeping the ashes away – why, it's then

I almost envy you that booby-trap.
All alive-o you strolled to pinch firewood
From the one innocent house that still stood
On Shoreham beach. You never knew what it meant
To look for blood in your daily excrement;
You never knew the mine that blew you up.

Grass

Whoever has travelled in grassless places
Remembers for ever the upward stare
Of blind earth eying out of pits
To gaze
A skull-face changeless over the bone.

I am thankful for the grass I own.
It clothes bare tilth that my
Deliberate seed refuses;
It grafts an
Unbidden skin over the permanent soil.

But I have known it fail:
Given as the snow, it is taken away
In arid summers. When evenings grow
Ungardenly
With broadcasts of oriental war,

I have stood at my open door
Remembering the wild rice of Asia
Teeming in waste, unpeopled swamps,
And the blanched
Lepers corroding through the cities.

Near them, where no grass is,
The slat-flanked cattle sometimes come,
Bringing a shrivelled cud gathered
From far off.
Rare seed falls on them from long-flighted birds.

A Place of Trees
(for Bernard Price)

They've been felling. From the copse
Beside the lane, all day long,
I have listened to the collapse
Of timber, the mad saw wailing

Agonized while it spun free,
And then the blade's grateful moan
As it cracked another tree
Like a dog splintering a bone.

Thinking I'd take a last look,
I came when the man had left.
In the failing light the smoke
Of their bonfires lingered soft

Among the wilting laurels
That used to grow in the dark.
The raw stumps were tar-barrels
Open to the shooting spark,

But by those flares I could recall
No individual trunk,
No limb, or any single
Leaf of what lived here. I think

In this winter night only
Of close, high-summer shadows
Gathering over a lonely
Visitor. A dirt path shows

The way he came to this place
Of trees. It leads into a dry
Field, and fields beyond, then space
Beyond the last star of the sky.

Hothouse

There was a place in his mind
where the man could be alone
from choice, free from his children
and not at home to his friend;
where husband was husbandman

not to be called to his food
but in his own time. He made
all weather that entered; took
rain from a pipe at the flood
or trickle, as the mood took

him. He could put out the sun
with lime-wash over the glass,
could waft on his leaves cool airs
at will. He saw a season
breed that was not the summer's,

all summer. He was a god
come to crucify his trees
on wires. Whatever would grow
would grow as he thought was good.
In winter he lit his fires

covertly in a furnace-house:
new stars to warm his planet.
Lamps left to burn through midnight
lit the sliding snow-waters
from the roof. He would delight

in visiting his blossom,
come spring, with a rabbit's scut.
Before the first bees were out,
busily his hands would swarm;
infallible crops would set.

When he bruised the ripened fruit,
he savoured an urgent juice
that spilled in his hand. The house
had swollen more than he could eat.
Nectarines were everyone's.

In an hour they would pick him bare
and leave goodbyes. He would stay
a little while, after. He
would be tired at the door
where the strange day-lilies sway.

Swallows

A day of winter-slaked April.
Bobbers on a wire at a wall –
trindles of fire-blued iron
that any wind twitches – twirl
and are lifted into swallows.

Little red particles of thirst,
the red summer of brickdust
are those throats among a month
avaricious of its damp; fust
of the whitening lichen,

buffed by delicate bellies,
comes live out of its ice.
Blue is warm of swallows' wings:
rich spillings of their sapphires
glint along the dark, nettled end

of garden. They are my claim –
over half a world they come,
crop-full of Africa, to lodge
in crevices of my home.
In honorance of such plenty,

I make them a plot of hotness
to skim upon: hibiscus,
hyssop, pools of buddleia,
a humming of mulberries.
I fork the brown mulch of one

summer less into my earth
as warm weather falls. Nothing can encourage their coming
again. I leave them be, with
an untouched, vulnerable clutch

of another year's small flesh.
Soon my eyes must relinquish
Them. When the hips are redder
than the roses were, they'll brush
my willow a final time,

flying out of the house.
And, a continent deep, I sense
some other self – between us,
paltry, diminishing oceans
and arid, vanishing land.

Kraaled in a vast and untried
veld, his sleep is troubled.
My wall of lichen relapses white.
In the night he lifts his head,
listening for ultimate swallows.

The Night Bathers

I walk, a stranger here,
in alien, emptying Wales
through orange montbretia
wild among fallen walls
of a left, profitless farm
where only visitors come.

Along the promontory
warm of an indolent lick
Of August water, hazes
close on a momentary crow.
Dark is a lenient harm
over Cardiganshire.

I am alone as now
my son is alone. Below
the headland he worries at sleep
where bushes breathe the evening
in. Troubles of honeysuckle
film his air. Remorse of mine

wrapped him about too warm;
he wrestled off my comforting.
A thunder sensed in other hills
has moved away. Rain would ease him
but it will not rain. All day,
as sands of little birds lifted

in a strapping summer wind
that smacked canvas brittle with sun,
I was aware of health and
used it bitterly in play,
pitiless against the man
growing from the sullen boy

rid of me now. I made him
run out the slack of the tide
till sand was dry on his tiredness
and the sea was a far, shut bud.
Now, as he ebbs in a dream
from the pull of my contrition,

I hear the night bathers come
over the yelping stones. I see
by astonishing bonfires
in an idleness of yachts
my father running down the beach
twenty grown years ago, at home;
when he was young to understand
why, momently out of the night
and purposeful beyond the reach
of all his worry, I had swum
deep into banks of sea-fret
too far to have to answer him.

From
Gloves to the Hangman
(Poems 1969-72)

O My Gentle Creatures (after Salvatore Quasimodo)

O my gentle creatures, now
the green that was in the hills
turns ruinous with autumn.
Once more before nightfall we
shall hear the birds' last lament
and call from the grey plain
rise toward the rumorous sea.
The scent of rain-wet wood, of
rabbit-burrows, here among
houses, among men, grows strong,
now, O my gentle creatures.

Slow eyes in this turning face,
this hand stretched toward heaven
where the ripping thunder is –
they belong to you, my wolves,
my blood-scorched foxes. All hands,
all faces, yours. And you tell
of futility, of life's
days worn as if by water
remorselessly away, while
in the garden children sing.
Far from us now, maybe? But
like shadows, less than shadows,
they slip to the air. This is
your voice. Yet perhaps I know
not everything has been.

A Celebration for Autumn
(for John Ormond)

Once more I welcome a purer darkness
Of evening in the hour of the year
Between summer and an end of summer,
When the soft air is songless as moss
Over the barn where the swallows are

Restless. Something has wearied the sun
To yellow the unmolested dust
On the bitter quince; something is lost
From its light, letting waxen bees drown
In their liquor of fatigue. But by last

Shadows of another season gone,
I live into beginning autumn
To see its silver, broken column
Of thready smoke ascending. Someone
Has gathered up his few leaves fallen

On the morning's webby lawn, who knows
Nothing of how I share them. I think
Of his hands at the live fire, and thank
Him in his private wood for what grows
Commonly for us toward the stars

I recognize of winter to come.
And I remember an August once,
With armfuls of slushing leaves, left since
Noon to dry by the hedge they fell from,
Shiny as the shears. Could we burn them

Now, I wheedled my grandfather, now?
Everything in its own due time,
He said, for fires need cold and autumn
Dark if you want their flowers to grow;
And who was I to call down the snow

Before its proper season? The weeks
Frittered on beyond the old man's dying,
And the ready pears, and my crying
In his garden-rows of empty sticks.
His fire shot higher than hollyhocks

One night when the smell of dead summer
Was too much to bear. It was for me,
Who had had hardly a breath easy
From the heavy hammer of asthma,
That frost assembled in that glimmer

Of thrown smoke, and prized into my blood
Like the feel of knives over the skin.
I lived on into its cold. Again
I tread through a crisping grass; the hard
Air closes again, and I am glad.

Some troubled sleep it may take to bear
The slump of one less summer – but clean
The sun tomorrow, or the frail rain.
I shall breathe in refreshed September.
I have much to thank my autumns for.

One Magpie for Sorrow

Now the rafters lift and shake
On blunt struts above the loft
And the flues whine down from the dark.
November again, month of my birth,
Blanches the stones bare to the earth

And gusts a single magpie, bereft
And cowering, to the stripped magnolia.
In my hearth the cold cinders shift
As I stare from the place where I belong.
Riffling another dying year, among

Dumb tokens of all I choose to be,
I pretend nothing can change. Yet,
As the day fades over the broken country
And this old white house prey to the weather,
I know my lie; know too well what other

Selves might enter. The magpie that
Cannot be hidden by darkness or by snow
Crouches under the wind. I shut out
Winter, whatever must come to pass.
Brittle twigs grint against the glass.

New Forest Ponies

They stopped from a gallop. Steam
left them like epiphanies
loose in the dusk. I saw them
whisking at snowflakes like flies.

It was a pair of forest
mares, briskets slung like hammocks
of fat matelots. With rapt lust
they browsed remnants of picnics

beside the Brockenhurst road.
Hobos, they rifled litter-bins,
turfing out chicken bones; then stood
casually among beer-cans,

posed for a snap-shot album.
I nudged them along the verge
until their stallion came
prancing a disremembered rage

through the ice twilight. His strength
was flagged, a softening thong
of wash-leather. The cushy south
where he lives, where I belong,

would paddock him for gymkhanas,
currying his fourteen hands
to a genteel handsomeness.
Now he smelt like failing ponds,

shut cinemas. He began to come
at me. Gripping the fence-post,
I waited. But he ambled, a tame
elderly man in tweeds, lost
in some reverie of war,
all wildness shrunk. White of eyes
was mush, the shown teeth sulphur
dull. He let me feel him – thews,

veins, worn cordage to the touch.
I held him grass on the palm.
He cadged himself a sandwich;
mooched away, slavering jam.

The Émigrés

Visiting from Britain, I take my ease
In a Massachusetts yard. Willows
Have opened overnight along the ridge;
This is the second spring I've seen this year.

I watch as my once-English hostess
Moves across the shadow of the spruces
At her door. She calls her home a cottage
And puts on homeliness like a sweater.

She's tried, over and over, to grow grass
Around the place; grass, and a few roses,
And even, look, a bit of privet hedge
To remind her of home in Warwickshire.

She brings me bourbon in an ice-packed glass
And tinkles on about the neighbours' houses.
Americanisms glint like a badge
Pinned onto her. She much prefers life here,

She protests, remembering what life was
For her in England – the dirt, rising prices,
Always having to live at the edge
Of her nerves. Not to mention the weather.

I stir my drink. 'I'd not mind it either,
For a while,' I say. Martins lodge,
Like swallows at home, in crevices
Of her roof. 'Oh, purple martins, those

Damn things. I'll have to rake them down from there,'
She says. 'Mind you, it's not that I begrudge
Them somewhere to live. But if you saw the mess
They make, you wouldn't think me heartless.'

Now in his office near a fall-out shelter
High over downtown Boston, husband Reg
Will be turning his calendar (English Views
In Summertime) into May. The two of us,

Last evening, swept the last of the winter
Cones into a heap. Outside his garage
Afterwards, he told me, watching the flames,
Of all his new, perpetual worries:

There's his job—they daren't have kids. And Russia.
And how he'll never keep with the mortgage.
Not to mention the droughts, the six-foot snows.
In the yard where nothing English ever grows.

Afterwards

Afterwards, we quarrel from love
And once again we are back
In our disparate bodies.
The room cools, almost darkness,

My fingers gripping the fallen quilt.
You lie as if at the edge of the sea,
The sun gone off the water.
Hair has the slipperiness of eelgrass.

Oh, the words you flung, I hear them,
Pebbles tumbling, smoothened with use;
But hurting; but individual; belonging
To us – worth keeping for themselves.

While you sleep, I gather them.
You shift. I listen for the city.
Tyre-hiss, a draining breakwater;
I remember finding a kittiwake, dead.

You are so cold. I should cover
This illicit skin awash in the moon.
I lift you as though you were mine
To keep. Let me see your eyes.

Letter to Marcel Proust

I

Monsieur, when I first met you (introduced
  by a Cambridge don eighteen years ago)
there wasn't much about you I cared for.
  Semites, I loathed, and next to Semites, queers;
never having fancied fellers, I fought off
  two-pound notes with a roustabout righteousness,
and duffed up a bent yid once with a wire brush.
  What's more, my father being a working bloke
who'd been on the dole through my 'thirties boyhood,
  I'd learned by heart to put grub before ethics,
so that the world of Albertine and Madame Verdurin
  unfolding between your punctilious semi-colons
wasn't, so to speak, du côté de chez moi.
  To one of my generation of yobbos
who had inherited the posher universities,
  all that palaver in scented drawing-rooms
was dated as Zeppelins, a right load of shite.
  We turned every snobbery upside-down
and parodied a life we never would live:
  (not for us the tea-time punt to Grantchester
but sooner a canoe to a pub in Trumpington).
  But, Thanks, mate, I told my broken supervisor,
bidding him tara with a wave of the ration-book
  that marked the page we'd got to in Swann.
One day you'll remember all this, he said,
  moithering off towards the Combination Room,
à la recherche du ton perdu.

II

Today, bombing southwards on Autoroute 6
  à mi-chemin between Paris and Lyon,
one of my bus-load of dumb Yankee students
  offered me a madeleine from a plastic bag.
Ever the pedagogue, I seized the opportunity
  to give my spiel (lasting 40 kilometres)
on the involuntary memory, monsieur, and you.
  Christ, what a drag – like, man, who needs it?
was what I got from the weirdo freak.

(Though later, at the zinc in the comfort-station
I smiled to observe that the woolly number
    was dunkin' a thoughtful Donut in a demi-tasse.)
Oh, the immutable ghastliness of students!
    Marcel (est-il permis?), I too am nostalgic
for the decencies of life I see in decay:
    I want no part of the acid-head commune
sharing out equally its bread and its crabs
    (any more than I'd want the return to privilege
and the tittling Tatler and its snaps of debs);
    yet maybe we're wrong to despair of the future,
its perspective of instant beds stretching end to end.
    There will always be those to share our snobbery
for what comes difficult, like Art and Love,
    and even (dare one mention it?) tolerance
by which, since Israel and the Wolfenden Report,
    hetero queer-bashing fascists like me
have learned, with time, to be friends with such as you.

From
Burning the Ivy
(Poems 1973-77)

Moving

Do not attempt to sleep – your strangeness
Arouses the new house. Amazed floors,
Unaccustomed yet to what is yours,
Shift to the burden of what you bring;
Overhead, the loft that encloses

A fresh store of sentimental junk
Creaks from your broken bits of childhood.
Sometimes maybe it's all to the good
To touch, to rearrange all you own
Elsewhere. But in someone else's sink,

Though it's yours now and paid for, even
A cup can remind you of who you are,
And what you were, and why you are here.
From choice, or by accident, or both,
Once more you've humped your stuff. The oven

Was worst, its squat, impervious bulk
Grudging each inch. Yet plain heaviness,
Lifted and lifted, doesn't oppress
Like those gross abstracts we can't dispose
Of. They arrive with the morning milk.

Ivy

Nine years ago I killed the ivy:
But once more it swarms the ancient wall
Round my plot. It had grown top-heavy
And rank, too much for the bricks to bear;
Powdery mortar has begun to fall

As fall it did our first winter here,
Eaten away by ravaging roots.
Ripened, the poison berries cluster;
Black swags in the February wind
Loom over my soil. A sleet shower starts

As I place the ladder, climb high and
Straddle the coping. Evergreen leaves
Conceal dust of dead seasons. I find
The wren's nest we hunted for one spring;
A ball; a lost doll that falls in halves

In my hands. Engrossed now, clambering
On, I incise with new secateurs
The tangle of years. Dismembering
Thick, reptilian stems, my palm bleeds;
I grasp sticky lushness. For the hours

It takes to shear clean my fifty yards
Of masonry, all is forgotten
Of what gnaws my present self. Last birds –
Rooks and lapwings – fly above a house
That once was not mine, will not be mine

One day; unfamiliar, those windows
Lit one by one and uncurtained yet
Against the dark. Another nine years
Another, someone must grub up trunks
As I tomorrow shall in the wet

Field outside the wall. A blunted axe
He'll bring back, whoever he may be.
As long as I hone its edge, I'll give thanks
For the task. Duly, as men have done
Their several times each century

Since the bricks were laid, one morning soon
I'll re-point the gaps creepers have picked
Between them. I'll watch my ivy burn,
Tendrils of flame clinging to the flat
Surfaces of night; will sense what hacked

Vines will grip again, cannot be kept out.

Elegy for an Old Acquaintance

Give sorrow words: the grief that does not speak
Whispers the o'erfraught heart, and bids it break.
                                                (Macbeth, IV, iii)

Before true autumn the sun
   has less warmth than flesh
and the days fall golden-green
   as the smooth rind of quinces;
to face into such sunlight
   is like bathing in milk.

And yet we have no name for
   the year's blandest interim
before the breath turns rancid
   in the mouth of October,
while the hours pour languidly
   upon themselves like oils.

Nor, as I hear you are dead,
   sometime, casual friend, have I
words for what is less than grief
   but more than common sorrow.
All our lives we prepare
   for the vaster bereavements:

every day, in case they die,
   I kill my children in my mind.
But no time is apt for the death
   of those we owe almost love –
a liking beyond affection;
   of those we seldom visit

but are always glad to see.
   our stored tears are not for them
whose lives are but particles
   not masonry of our own.

Their elegies are for ourselves,
   our parings, out bits of dead
skin. It is a nameless season
   of small mourning the heart keeps

every day that comes. I would wish
   to name its tart fruits of regret:
whatever it is we feel, making
   acknowledgement of minor loss,
of meagre failure, of yielding
   to time what was ours for good;

what shall we call those calendars
   of all unmemorable decay?
Old friend, if I speak no grief,
   yet know I am not untouched
by what you do so untimely.
   They are yours, the small, final

roses opening scentless in my garden.
   I spend an empty afternoon
watching the summer's end; this air
   I breathe from the quenches stubble-
fires fusts on the lung. It is for all
   us living, inarticulate, small

sorrowers my heart lurches now
   as I gag towards the sun;
for us all notice the lichen
   on the wall bounding what is mine
and sense what feeble, savage-rooted growths
   pick at the fabric of happiness.

Between Acts

Worthing, the nineties; pier and promenade
Busy with bathchairs, wicker bassinets.
An upper window in the Esplanade
Releases smoke of scented cigarettes.

In this lacklustre town a masterpiece
Takes shape. Elsewhere, with all the earnestness
Of being unimportant, grim police
Take evidence. So does a mad marquess.

But play, as well as The Play, must go on.
In a hired boat, and 'rented' for the day,
The author dallies down to Littlehampton.

So, bathing in fame and briny on the way,
Hubristic yet, and yet to be reviled,
Sails Oscar Fingall O'Flahertie Wills Wilde.

Perfidious Euterpe

I

Where does she keep? Assume her
among fusted arcana

in the mind's loft. The bitch
muse has her hair liced as cottage-thatch.

Brittle as mouse-bone, her nails.
Her skin's the grey of dead gulls.

He remembers her pure white
before she learned to abort

with a filthy spike;
who sang with him once, awake

with child, feckful yet the sun,
and he not any kept man.

Nightly he gropes up
to her through the attic trap

of dreams. His mornings smell
like bleach on a hot blanched wall.

II

Four times a year she stirs him
to stare, glad from a window
and say, This is my season.

March, it was an only snow
he glimpsed, like a pinch of moths;
In June, the scarlet beanflower

was nudged by bees; a pheasant
craked out of the first mauve hour
of Michaelmas; and an owl

creatured from December light
clung like a corbel under
his eaves. Always the glass clouds

over, though from the sigh of
joy. When he rubs his wrist
congealed and fouling breath

glairing the millimetres
between him and the insight
of fragments of happiness,

a left-behind glaze distorts
like oil on fresh rainwater.
Summer, spring, winter and fall

finish, within the minute
of their beginning. The world
worsens, traduced with tears.

Rivers

Bridges are rare over still water.
Lagoons and lakes offering
 no grain to work against, we
circumambulate lengthily
 but without rancour. Tactful
roads, visiting soon leave
 at arbitrary tangents. No –
like mountains, lakes and lagoons
 don't seem to stand in our way:
containing within themselves
 the weight of all their gallons,
they keep a place that is theirs.
 Swiftly we cross a skiff.
See how an expert oarsman
 leaves prints on the waterskin
where piers would support the bridge
 thrown by a megalomaniac.

Your river, though, is hostile.
 Whereas brooks, rivulets
accept the simple homage
 of two thick planks or a tree
felled or fallen, your river
 makes insufferable demands.
Below where you may ford, vault,
 leap or stepping-stone across
you must gawk at the far shore.
 With that satisfaction one
would straddle the Amazon,
 stooping to drink from its source!
Aping the caveman you can
 swim, raft it over on logs …
Hire mathematicians, else:
 equations to do with bridges
are several inches long.

Beneath their arches congregate
all manner of disruptives
    (lovers, derelicts, suicides,
the planters of gelignite)
    while upright citizens cross
purposeful as salmon.
    At nightfall, ruminative,
old men use parapets of bridges
    to lean from and gob. Black
silkweed streams from cutwaters,
    grips, is gone. Unfinishing,
rivers are always elsewhere.
    Wade them after dark, cast
somewhere into their hissing,
    feel how they clasp your thighs
as though they were the drowners.
    See them slide under your shadow.

Wild Bird in a Living Room

It means bad; starling
a slam and a slam
at the glass. We're shut
in a gadarene house,

our faces white from
a street accident.
We want it to die,
to shovel it out.

But it clutches books,
stabs the taut vellum
of a lampshade, drips
ticks from its soot feathers.

Its brittling legs
are a filth. Should we leave,
like all afternoon
restless on a beach,

dried seaweed skirring
like flocks in the mind?
We stay, watching, grip
till light sucks it out,

fumble for the window-catch.
The room is exorcised.
Clean birds sparkle the grass.
We weep with sanity.

Vipers,

sliding, pour themselves through themselves,
bits of miniature rivers.

Slack else, still
as worry beads left where they fell,

they abrade the young year's sun
in grit, green, brick, stucco brown,

a crumble. Always the eyes, coppery red –
sometimes the tongue, loose threads

flickering the wind.
This one I found

dead today, coils in a coil,
fills its Chinese bowl

with spent resilience. I'll keep it
as long as this takes to write.

Never before did I own a viper. Touch,
flinch,

to remember dry heaths of boyhood
summer, brackens, the sandy birchwood,

yelping in a pack for the hated snake –
deadly adder. With a fork-ended stick

you'd fix his wriggling, knife his
sin. It was the lore of boys:

make a belt of the skin, heat
the flesh in an iron pan for the fat

that cures deafness.
Older, with a first girl in the sharp, dark grass,

you listened for the swift sibilance
of adders, appalled; and appalled in the silence

after, still you'd listen.
But, since you've seen them often,

commonplace on an afternoon path,
exotic, arcane, tempting as death

to disturb. Several, zigzagged, ravelled as whips
lashed round themselves, whirls and loops,

finally subsided, a muddled tie-drawer.
One, disentangling, sloughed like a whore

peeling a stocking back. The new
head, mint as a pebble damped with dew,

had to be smashed. This one that's mine,
stiff in its small blood, its venom mine

for the simple milking, could kill
from posthumous spite. Did Adam, some residual

innocence left him in his great age,
life the serpent's carcass in homage

to the nighthawk?
In the garden, to the dark

I commit this thing.
The fang

feels like red wire. I'd have
let this one live.

From
Mangoes on the Moon
(Poems 1992-98)

First Night In Australia

When young, I never asked why it should be
My right hand in the mirror was his left;
He was other; he was a different me
Laterally (not vertically) cleft.

Then, adult, I became mildly disturbed
To read of doppelgänger. Some girl said,
'You have a double.' Other-self-absorbed,
I wondered if he would go out of his head

If he met me. Sci-fi, in middle-age,
Acquainted me with 'anti-matter'. I,
Homme moyen sensual, inclined to rage
At bosh, discounted this as all my eye.

I'm not sure of that now I've grown old.
I'm often not myself. Jet-lagged I lay
Sleepless in bed last night; the darkness told
The mind of night that body felt was day.

Orion strangely stood upon his head;
Noon sun had been due north; water had drained
Counter-clockwise from the bath. Being dead,
Perhaps, might feel something like this: ingrained

Knowledge somehow being turned upside down,
Or back-to-front, or inside-out – all three,
Maybe, at once. And so I rose, and with a frown
I rushed to ascertain there was a me

Reflected still. Above the bathroom shelf
The glass did reassure. And yet not quite:
In hot December, was that other self
Sweating to tell his left hand from his right?

For His Second Wife

We dream our earlier loves. Yes,
In shared separateness
We both weep, remembering
Some unrepeatable kiss,
Our dear dead revisiting
Unannounced but welcome
Always to enter this home.

Would they accuse? Would they
Think it our treachery –
Even though they are long gone –
To comfort body with body?
And can a woman and a man
Begin again (it's selfish
To survive) if not with flesh?

In almost contiguous graves
And under promiscuous leaves
They lie closer than we,
Forever unaware how love's
Nature outlives jealousy.
With no option we draw breath,
Pre-enacting guiltless death

In sleep. I have grown slow;
But clutch me before we go
To different rooms. Feel my face
One final time, as into
Chaste and uncorporeal space
We take, together and apart,
Our one, ageing, wiser heart.

For His Father

Father, when you lay dying,
And had grown threadbare-thin –
No more than your very bones
In a see-through bag of skin –
I sat beside you, crying,
Unable to bear your groans.
You'd given up defying,
Knowing you could not win.

Some strength you must have had
For, as our tension grew,
Aware we'd never meet again,
You were my stalwart who
Suffered me to kiss you, glad
To close weary eyes and then,
When I whimpered, 'Love you, Dad,'
Whispered, 'I know you do.'

Impasse

To long ago to matter,
The hurts my younger mother
Gave before I learned what
Love was. Yet

When I fret all night
Mithering that she nurtures hate
With little left except to die,
It's not the way

Her older self defies my love
That sours the final lees I have
So much as that
She it was who conceived it.

For Andrew Young

More often than ever we used to meet
I come across you, call you by the name
I never used to your living face: Andrew.
In gardens running to old roses, daphne
Mezereum, under my breath I speak it
As though you'd plunged only for moments
Into some shrubbery gloom beyond the lawn.

For then you'd appear, lead us all indoors
From final sun, blackbird song, japonica –
Men and women cast as ladies and gentlemen
In that room of fragile talk, blue-rimmed china.
In your house I was never easy. Me it was
You chose to process behind your slippered shuffle
To some unlit antre where our smoking occurred.

While your Woodbine ash lengthened and drooped
But would not fall to soil your clerical chest,
Ignorance burned inside me; and stray wisps
Of stupidity dried my discomfited lips.
'What do you know of Prehistory?' you offered,
handing me matches to light an electric fire;
and I groped for flex, for facts, until you said,

'There's almost nothing anybody knows.'
I wanted you to think well of me. Once,
In a pheasant-crawling wood near my home,
A hundred miles east of common rarity
I'd flushed the wild flower, *Paris Quadrifolium.*
I would have let fall this trivium, had you not said,
Before my chance, you'd noted Herb Paris

In my village years before my birth.
Our long, shared, comfortable silences
Were best. An hour and ten minutes we sat
In my car outside your gate, being together.
Back from the hospital where Mrs Young
Still answered to the name of *I say.*
Around her bed the ward floor was strewn

With hairpins like a hatching of craneflies;
And you had been outraged that I, a man,
Should willingly have entered a shop to buy
A new brood of hairpins. It took that long,
I guess, for you not to have to say, and for me
To sense, that a kindness can be forgiven:
You made me take the threepence that you owed.

And, since you stumped away for good, often
I seem to have watched you go; caught one glimpse
Of you a blink before you disappeared
Over a hill, or into a copse of trees;
Not far ahead, no further than the stars,
No longer ago than Prehistory, you, close,
Remote, loved, unknowable companion, Andrew.

Paper Windmills

'Molinos de Papel? There's nothing there,'
She said, and slapped my change down on the bar.
In my mind's eye I saw the summer air
Troubling some paper windmills. 'Is it far?'

I asked, 'I'd like to go.' She tossed her hair
In disbelief and scorn. 'You have a car?'
'Well, no,' I said. 'I'll walk. The day is fair.'
And so I trod for hours through melting tar,

Found nothing but deserted pulping mills –
If "nothing" may include a house or two
With foaming roses at the window sills

Above a patio where a couple sat.
White petals filled with wind. Nothing to do
But leave, I watched some fall, settled for that.

Driving Through Orange Groves

Among so many millions there was one tree
That momentarily filled my driver's eye, one
I'd never find again – though I saw every leaf
Individual, glossed slick and wetly fresh
From a lavishing brush: dark, a looming-green.

Not a tree in full fruit, mind, not ponderous-
Boughed, not luminous by Christmas dusk,
Bespangled hours before picking-time; no, nor
Newly-blossomed, drenched in the scent
That fills a whole valley, even to over-spill the lip.

Time was, days long lost amid the dark groves,
When I'd have braked, stopped the engine, looked
Hard for hard, sour little oranges concealed among
The lacquered, evergreen swags; when all was
Unfinished orchard, for ever memorable. Not now.

From
"Love Songs from Castile"
(Previously Unpublished Poems c. 1979)

Celibate

No, the nights aren't easy.
I work as late as I can,
hearing other shutters rattle
while heat sifts like bran
through the slats I'm too lazy
to open wide. I might settle
for an hour with a book,
but mostly do no more than scan
a paragraph. I look
through your letters, breezy
with news but sad, and fan
myself with one. No, the nights
aren't easy. I undress
while I sip a glass of wine,
remembering how cool as cress
our room, when the streetlights
refresh your pillow and mine.
I turn back my sheet a little way
stretch in my bed's emptiness
and think of when you lay
with me last. On the heights
above this town, in a wilderness
of rock, monks are at prayer
while I wait for words from wordless air.

Hierbas Buenas

Why should it be that the blue rosemary flower
Should enter my head this midnight, I do not know.
I came from the bodega, my face moistened with rain,
And when my skin was dry and taut over the cheekbones
And I shut my eyes for sleep to come, the flower was there.

If there is rosemary here, still I have seen none.
Lavender you see; and of an evening in the public gardens,
Old people amble, sniffing a pinch of mint.
Yesterday, in the Church of Cristo del Amparo,
I picked up a sprig of thyme and wore it home.

We've always said we'd have a bunch of rosemary.
Had we planted it then, when first we said we would,
By now it would have been gaunt and leggy in the stem.
While I am away, reserve an autumn place for one.
It seems important. We've time for some bushes more.

Above Cuenca

(for Lorna)

How far it is from cliff to cliff
I could not tell you: but no voice
could carry the space from crag to crag,
no matter that the wind would lift it
like some petal high over the chasm.

You on your far side might also shout
and signal, seeing me signal wildly;
and sense how, somewhere in that void
(in the warm air rising from the river
where no one may listen) voices would meet.

Listen, this morning, down in the valley,
I sat by the water among the flowering limes.
In those woods there were more nightingales
than sparrows in our garden. I'd as well
have tried numbering the river's syllables

in the gurgling pink pebbles of its bed.
Here they call the birds ruiseñores
in the finishing trill you hear a word like niña.
After an hour of them, I could take no more.
I crossed the bridge, climbed to the open air;

where I have been all day, staring across.
Were you here, after the last of the sun,
watching the ravening flight of the swallows,
I should tell you their name golondrina
which now I whisper into the ravine.

To shout would be pointless; to keep silence
while the birds wheel and scream, too uneasy.
Tonight, while I telephone, they'll grip their cliff,
This side, that side, between them a rising
lime-blossom scent depriving the last of emptiness.

From
Grandad's Seagulls
(Children's Poems 1994)

Awake

Those awesome noises of the night
All bring an element of fright
To make me welcome morning light.

How eerily the hound-dog howls
From far-off darkness full of owls
And foxy prowlings after fowls.

I hear those ambulances wail
Up distant hill, down distant dale,
Telling a sad pathetic tale.

The gunmen of the street conspire
To murder me: how I perspire,
Startled, if worn-out cars backfire.

The wind is in my apple-tree;
Its branches whisper breathily
That they are coming after me.

Something in the house is thrumming
Can it be nocturnal plumbing?
No – a breathing someone's coming.

Pummel pillows, try as I might,
Twisting ropes of bedclothes tight
I can't expunge my second-sight.

What are those shapes? I can't be sure.
My wardrobe creaks. A tapping door,
Scuttling creatures under the floor.

And scratchings in my attic scare
Because I fancy harm is there
Embodied forms from empty air.

The black of night turns pearly grey;
Come quickly, light, come quickly, day,
Wipe all my terrors clean away.

An Old Rook

O, you bit of broken black umbrella!
In an ancient gown, all rags and tatters,
You flop like a poor down-and-out fella
Among the scraps of yesterday's dinner;
And while that show-off, the magpie, chatters
And shouts the odds, and brags like a sinner,

Strutting about in his tight skinny suit,
You gather together about your ribs
The outfit you wore as a young recruit,
Too voluminous now and shot to ribbons.
With comical dignity, pace among the dribs
And drabs that the starlings, gibbering like gibbons,

Ignore. Now, then: stab that chicken I curried,
And goose-step away. Lift off, unhurried.

Blackbird

Of all my morning choir
Most magical performer, O, you
At the tip-top twig of sycamore,
You miracle worker, pure flautist
And boy soprano rolled into one, you
Throbbing little body so bursting full,
You of the lovely liquid throat,

O, the golden bill, of the hard bright eye,
O, be the delight of an April sunshine,
Singing for all of us, over and over,
Dressed in brand-new, smart black cassock
To triple-note the glory of the spring!

Goldfish in the Garden Pond

Basking close to the sun as they are able,
They turn the afternoon into a fable:
Spillings of rich coins on a miser's table.

Acknowledgments

We would like to thank the Research and Employer Engagement Office at the University of Chichester for the grant that made this book possible.

We would also like to thank Wendy Ellison at the University of Chichester Library for her help and assistance with the Ted Walker Archive.

We are grateful to Leila Dewji of Sheil Land Associates Ltd for help in negotiating with Ted Walker's Literary Estate for permission to reproduce this selection of his poetry.

Additional thanks are due to the Chi Poets Group for their support with this project.

Finally, a special debt of gratitude is to due to Chris Anderson and Roy Donaldson for their work, help and advice in the production of this volume.

English at Chichester

The English Department at Chichester is one where critics, literary theorists and practising writers work directly alongside each other. We believe that this gives you a breadth of insight into language, literature and your own writing. Many of our students go on to publish and win prizes

We offer the following courses:

BA English
BA English & Creative Writing

MA Creative Writing

MPhil, PhDs available in:

English Literature
Creative Writing
Life Writing

The University's English team came 10th out of 104 nationally for student satisfaction. The University's English and Creative writing team came 5th out of 28 nationally for student satisfaction in relation to 'imaginative writing'.

We welcome applications from all prospective students. In addition to sixth-form students completing A-level studies or equivalent, we also welcome applications from mature students currently completing Access programmes, and are fully committed to considering other mature students with non-standard entry qualifications.

To find out more, please contact us on tel: (01243) 816002, email: admissions@chi.ac.uk or visit our website.

www.chiuni.ac.uk/english